D1496700

LET US ALONE

By
William R. Ervin

9780915447008

Illustrated by
Stephanie Kaye Ervin

ISBN # 0-915447-00-2

CONTENTS

ILLUSTRATIONS
by Stephanie Kaye Ervin

'To the student of our political and constitutional history it is strange how stubborn historical facts are quietly set aside and inferences and assumptions are used as postulates for huge governmental theories. These errors are studiously perpetuated, for in prescribed courses of reading in civics and history are books full of the grossest misstatements teaching sectional opinions and latitudinous theories, while works which present opposite and sounder views are vigorously excluded.'

Hon. J.M.L. Cury, **Secession and the Civil War**, p.5.

A short treatise on Florida history with primary emphasis on the early Indian cultures to the Second Seminole War. This work is dedicated to all those men and women who believed in and fought for their land against all odds.

GENERAL REMARKS

This compiling of official and unofficial records, plus personal observations and study could not have been accomplished without the assistance of my wife, Dorothy Lee Ervin, who understood my admiration of our heritage and never once hindered me in my efforts to study our nation's past.

It is almost impossible to loosen a person's heartstrings, which bind him to another person or to the land. Once they are loosened the person changes in some way, and if the heartstrings are severed something within that person dies. He tries to fill this void caused by the loss of one loved by stimulants, whether it be drugs, alcohol or tobacco, but the void is never filled. The Indians of Florida and North America, had their heartstrings torn many times from what they loved and they never recovered.

Even though this is primarily about Florida, the states which border her are also involved. When I became associated with living history programs with other members of the Historic Florida Militia, I found that information regarding early Florida history was not readily available. To research this time period the individual had to search through many monographs to obtain needed information. All the information herein has been taken from reputable sources and these have been noted in the resource section. At times I have had to make logical deductions to reach some conclusions of which I found no record. For example, during the Creek War in Alabama I found no reference to General Jackson making a stirring speech to his troops exhorting them to remain. However, knowing the spirit of the time and reading about the political and legal (for Jackson was a lawyer)

makeup of General Jackson I felt it safe to assume that he would first exhort his volunteers before threatening to shoot them.

The title, '**Let Us Alone**', is taken from the words that appeared on the first flag of Florida. Even though this state flag was not officially approved by the Florida Legislature, it did fly over the inauguration of the state's first governor, Governor Mosely. The flag was raised, and flown, just this one time on July 4th, 1845, when Florida officially entered the roll call of states and the twenty-seventh star was added to the flag of the United States. This unofficial state flag consisted of five horizontal stripes; blue, orange, red, white and green. Emblazoned brightly across the second stripe were the words 'LET US ALONE.' As there were no pictures made of this flag, the description varies with the different accounts read. Some writers say the motto was in a different location while some writers say that in the left hand upper corner of the flag was a blue field with stars representing the various states of the union. Other writers state that in the upper left hand corner of the flag was a small United States flag. One thing all the writers of the period are agreed on is the motto. This flag, with its motto 'LET US ALONE,' was symbolic of all people everywhere who are fiercely independent.

History is a grouping of facts, and sometimes fiction, written from the viewpoint of the writer and the victors. I have learned that only those who fought in the trenches can judge those who are in the trenches. For as Jesus said: 'Do not judge, or you will be judged. For in the same way you judge others, you will be judged, and with the measure you use, it will be measured to you.'

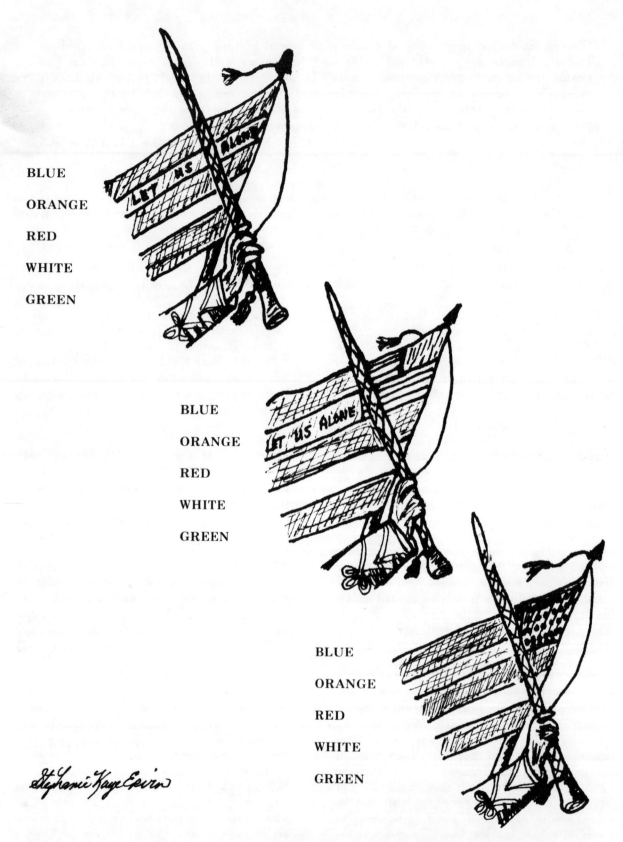

BLUE

ORANGE

RED

WHITE

GREEN

BLUE

ORANGE

RED

WHITE

GREEN

BLUE

ORANGE

RED

WHITE

GREEN

Renditions of some of the descriptions of the first Florida flag. According to some sources the color sequence in the second flag is blue, white, red, white and green. What these colors represent we do not know.

4

ACKNOWLEDGEMENTS

There were many people who have freely given of their time and energy to assist me in this work. Quite frequently, while conversing with them regarding Florida and her heritage, I was given information or leads regarding little known aspects of Florida. Some of the information was easily included in this book, other information regarded a different time period and some I would not think of including in anything. In following the leads concerning this time period I would at times come to a complete dead end; other times I followed the lead, as through a maze, and would find answers which either completely repudiated or exonerated that which I have been taught. There was also some information found which left me undecided on what really happened.

Special words of thanksgiving must be addressed to the following who aided me immeasurably. William Hart allowed me access to his law library and assisted me in locating documents pertaining to the late seventeenth and early eighteenth centuries. Allene Baus, Central Florida Chapter Historic Florida Militia, read through many rough drafts and showed me areas which needed modification or amplification. Some of these areas had to be dropped, not because they were uninteresting to me, but because I could not find any way to substantiate what I had found. Arthur Baus, Central Florida Chapter Historic Florida Militia and member of the Orange County Historical Society, allowed me free rein to pick his brain for any of his great wealth of knowledge of the British and Spanish period in the Floridas. He also gave me unlimited access to his library for any additional material. Rosemary Still, History Department, Volusia County School System, proofread sections of the rough draft. She offered many valuable suggestions and comments regarding various aspects of life in early Florida. Elisabeth Evans, secretary for William Hart, did all the final typing. I watched her working on a draft of this one day and I was amazed at how she was able to do it. Without the assistance of each one of these individuals, this project would never have gotten past a first draft stage. Yet when the final card is played the responsibility for all mistakes and errors rests with me.

THE SLIPPY STONE

Go carefully through this weary world,
And pick your steps with care,
And never do your neighbor wrong,
But always do what is fair,
Men fall and never rise again,
Who never fell before:
There's always a very slippy stone,
At everybody's door.

And if your neighbor chance to fall.
You must not let him lie,
But give a hand to help him up,
As you are passing bye.
The case may be your own someday
Though guides you have in store
There's always a very slippy stone
At everybody's door.

There's slippy stones wherever you go,
By cottage, hut and hall,
And you must pick your steps with care,
Or over them you may fall.
For Emperors and Kings have fallen,
By the score,
There's always a very slippy stone,
At everybody's door.

Go cannily and watch your step
And dinna cease to pray
That He who guides the sun and stars,
Will help you on your way.
Step by step He'll lead you safe
And from His boundless store,
He'll help you o'er each slippy stone
Right up to Heaven's door.

*Translated from the Celtic by
John McGrath*

PRELUDE

In 1513 Ponce de Leon, sailing his ships along what is now the east coast of Florida, sighted a large inlet. Entering this inlet, later known as Mosquito Inlet and now called Ponce Inlet, he anchored his vessels and set foot on Florida soil. Where three rivers joined together he erected a cross and claimed all the land in the name of the king of Spain. As the joining of the three rivers seemed to form a cross he named the place 'Rio de la Cruc' or Rivers of the Cross. While resting his men and replenishing their supplies he was attacked by Indians and forced to withdraw. As it was during the Easter season (Pasqua Florida) that he landed, Juan Ponce de Leon named his discovered land La Florida.

According to the romantic view - the view of the real estate salesman of 150 years ago - Florida

> thy forests are virgin an inviolate; verdant thy savannas; thy groves as fragrant as ever - those perfumed groves of aniseed and orange, of myrtle and magnolia. Still sparkles upon thy plains the cerulean ixia; still gleam in thy waters the golden nymphae; above thy swamps yet tower the colossal cypress, thy gigantic cedar, the gum, and the bay tree; still over thy gentle slopes of silvery sand wave long leafed pines, mingling their acetalous foliage with the frondage of the palm.[1]

Contrasting this view of the beauties of Florida we have the record of Secretary of War John C. Breckinridge. During the summer of 1865 he travelled along the western part of Volusia County on the St. Johns River. He and his party went up to the headwaters of the St. Johns, then across the Southern part of Volusia County to the Indian River, then south to the Indian River Inlet. Secretary Breckinridge, in his diary for May, 1865, wrote of the intense heat and humidity, the razor sharpness of many of the plants, the alligators and snakes. But his strongest attacks were on the mosquitos —

> I can not give you any adequate idea of these insects, they attacked us, not two or three at a time, but in swarms incessantly the whole night long. Both hands were kept going and still they bit us. With his arms tied and his face exposed, I am sure they would kill a man in two nights.

Dr. M. S. Jarvis, in his diary of the Seminole War, wrote on December 17, 1837:

> Nothing could equal the beauty of this forest. Of dense foliage composed of the Bay, Live Oak, Palmetto, Cypress and Cedar excluded every ray of sun and in the burning noonday heat of this climate must afford a delightful retreat. . . . The wild orange trees laden with fruit imparted a delightful fragrance to the air . . .[2]

A few days later, December 26, he writes:

> I rode into Powell town which is on the opposite side of the creek fronting our camp, but was obligated to make a speedy retreat from the immense swarms of fleas. In five minutes both myself and horse

were literally covered with them.[3]

And again in the entry for January 22, l838, we find:

> During the days several immense rattle snakes were killed by the soldiers none being under 5 feet in length. Those noxious reptiles became more numerous as we proceed south. One struck at a soldier in passing and entangled his fangs in his pantaloon and the first notice he had of his proximity was something that prevented his advancing his foot when looking behind for the cause he beheld a rattle snake of 6 foot long hanging on him.[4]

Dr. Ellis Hughes, in his diary regarding life in Florida during the Seminole War, writes:

> On horseback and dashing ahead with a will, I rejoiced that the fleas could not catch me - farewell Fort Hanson with thy warm cypress yellow spring water . . . thy flied sugar and fly-ed butter . . . farewell thy flies and sand bugs - mosquito and red bugs, my skin itches to think of you - farewell ye Florida forest vermin - I'm now for city life again.

After that Dr. Hughes left the St Johns River area for a brief rest in beautiful St. Augustine. In a later entry, the one for February 12, 1839, he writes:

> Tuesday evening found us at the 5 points of New River, a most beautiful stream with points as regular as a line of soldiers. With so beautiful a stream - so rich in vegetation, so numerous the game and so abundant the alimentary coontie and so delightful a climate no wonder the Indian clings to his own country.[5]

In 1696 Jonathan Dickinson was shipwrecked on the east coast of Florida. He kept a journal recording the adventures of his party as they walked and rowed from the Jupiter Inlet area to Charleston. He mentions one time when it got so cold with the northern winds that after building an evening fire some of his party dug holes in the sand and buried themselves. He further mentioned that the sand fleas and mosquitos were so numerous that his party could not rest that night but had to continue moving.

As can be seen by these early accounts, Florida was covered by beautiful underbrush and delightful overhanging foliage, yet intermingled with the ground covering and the trees were vermin, insects and reptiles of all sizes and shapes. Florida was also a hunting and fishing paradise for the early inhabitants. Through this forest primaeval wandered herds of bison, bear, fleet footed deer and other game. Rabbits and squirrels were in abundance; flocks of birds filled the air. The waters in and around the Florida Peninsula teemed with fish and shellfish of all descriptions.

In almost every account of travel in Florida during the period of exploration and colonization we find references to the marsh and swamp lands. Many of the diaries and records written during the second Seminole War record soldiers wading through water up to their chests.

Also in the reports written concerning the preparing of the plantations along the Mosquito River Area (Halifax River)

Figure 2

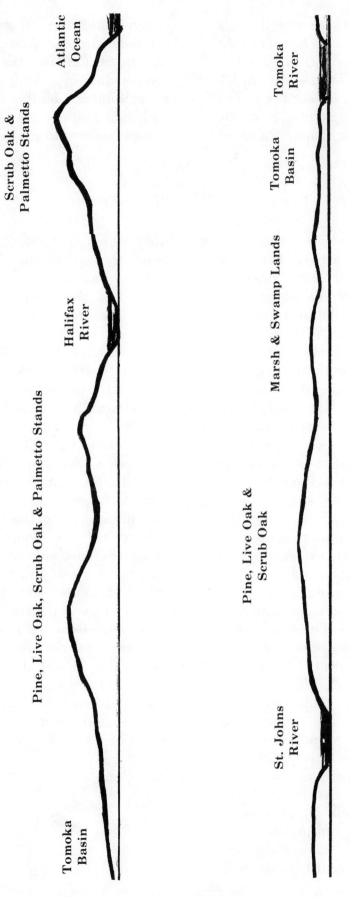

Cross section of Mosquito (Volusia) County from the Atlantic Ocean to the St. Johns River area showing general vegetation and type land.

9

to produce goods, there are always remarks about the workers having to dig drainage ditches or canals so the plantation would not be constantly flooded. These lowlands of eastern Florida were not only conducive to the planters for growing sugar cane or indigo, they were also good breeding grounds for the insects and vermin which so plagued the early settlers. Even today, by taking an airplane ride over Volusia County, it can easily be seen how marshy the land is. (Figure 1 shows cross section of Volusia County.)

GENESIS

How the early inhabitants - the Indians - of Florida arrived here and what their numbers were we have no concrete idea. It is estimated by some sources that the population numbered anywhere from ten to fifty thousand people. According to some anthropologists, the native inhabitants from 1500 to 1800 A.D. fell under the cultural influence of the Mississippian Moundbuilders. This means that the tribes or confederations of tribes in the Southeastern United States, including Florida, had similar economy, arts, crafts, religion, caste system, and passage rites.

As this culture existed during the days of the early European explorations of the 'New World,' we have many records of how the people appeared, their religion, their caste system, and all other aspects of their society. The survivors of De Soto's expedition described the members of this culture as having straight black hair, dark brown eyes and bronze colored skin. The men stood around 5 feet 10 inches tall, with the women's height a few inches shorter. Other early explorers amplified the discription by saying the men were handsome in appearance and the women were beautiful. There was no mongoloid cast to the appearance of any of the Indians in their culture, showing that they were a different heritage from the Indians of the western part and the northern parts of the United States.

When the first European explorers arrived on the Florida Peninsula, they found the area inhabited by six major tribes or confederations. The largest of these was the Timucuans, who ranged from the northeastern part of the state to south of the present day Daytona Beach. To the west they ranged from around the Aucilla River on the gulf coast south to near Tampa Bay. The Ais were located just below Daytona Beach and went south to the Cape Canaveral area. They went as far west as the St. Johns River. Just to the south of the Ais was located a tribe called the Jeagas. They ranged along the east side of the Everglades. Just below them and going to the tip of the Peninsula were the Tekestas, another loose knit tribe. Along the west coast of the Peninsula and up to near the Tampa Bay area were the Calusas. It was this tribe that wreaked havoc on Ponce de Leon's men. They also were the ones who killed that valiant explorer. In the northern part of the state in the panhandle area were located the Apalachees.

Florida Indian Cultural Aspects Relative to Other Native Cultures

The tribes which were associated with the Mississippian Culture are said to have achieved the highest cultural level of any North American Indian tribal group prior to the coming of the European. It 'was the immediate antecedent of the sophisticated southeastern chiefdoms - the Choctaw, Chickasaw, Natchez and others - that so impressed early explorers . . .'[6] It is thought that the arrival and encroachments of the white man caused this culture to lose its religious cohesiveness and split into the various tribes of the Southeastern United States. The culture of the Florida Indians was contemporary with the last 300 years of the Mayan Civilization on the Yucatan Peninsula. Also the Toltecs and the powerful Aztec Civilization existed entirely during the time of Mississippian Moundbuilder Culture. (Figure 2) The exact origin of the basis for the Florida Indian and the Mississippian Culture is not known for certain by archaeologists. However, it is known that this culture overlaps other advanced Indian cultures. It is also known that the water currents in the Gulf of Mexico flow past the Temple Building Mayan Culture on the Yucatan Peninsula. These currents flow directly onto the southern portion of the Florida Indian Culture. Archaeologists know that the Mayans used large three masted dugouts in their trading expeditions. In 1502 Bartholomew Columbus sighted dugouts far from the Yucatan Peninsula, in the Gulf of Mexico. Also there was lively trading between the various central American tribes and the tribes inhabiting the Greater and Lesser Antilles. With the ocean currents and the large trading dugouts favoring it, there was nothing to stop cultural diffusion from Central America to the Florida Peninsula area. (Figure 2A shows primary current in the Gulf of Mexico.)

The tribal confederations within the Southeastern United States were culturally bound together by their worship of the serpent, sun and eagle. This worship was carried out on mounds which were specially constructed for that purpose. This worship and the trade necessary to support it bound these people together. These tribes, being self-sufficient and bound together by religion and trade, were not war oriented, as were the Aztecs of Mexico. Even though they could be fierce warriors, they seldom fought within their confederation or with tribes outside their group. (Figure 3 shows early Southeastern tribes within the Moundbuilder Culture.)

As their domain contained much of the hardwood forest of the United States, they had ample water and game. Their land was truly a hunter's paradise. The trade, the agricultural surplus combined with the hunting and fishing, supplied all their needs and gave them time to develop artistic tendencies. In this development they had various economic groups, including pottery makers, metal workers, weapon and tool makers and a religious priesthood.

Economy

It is only in those cultures which have a substantial agricultural or food base that we find the economic situation such that the people have time to pursue aesthetic pastimes. Within the Southeastern portion of the United

11

Figure 2

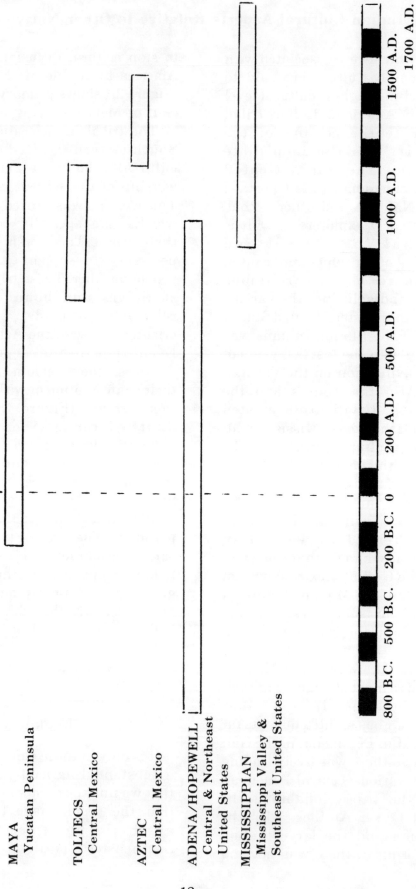

Approximate Time Graph of Major Indian Cultures in Central and Eastern North America.

12

Figure 2A

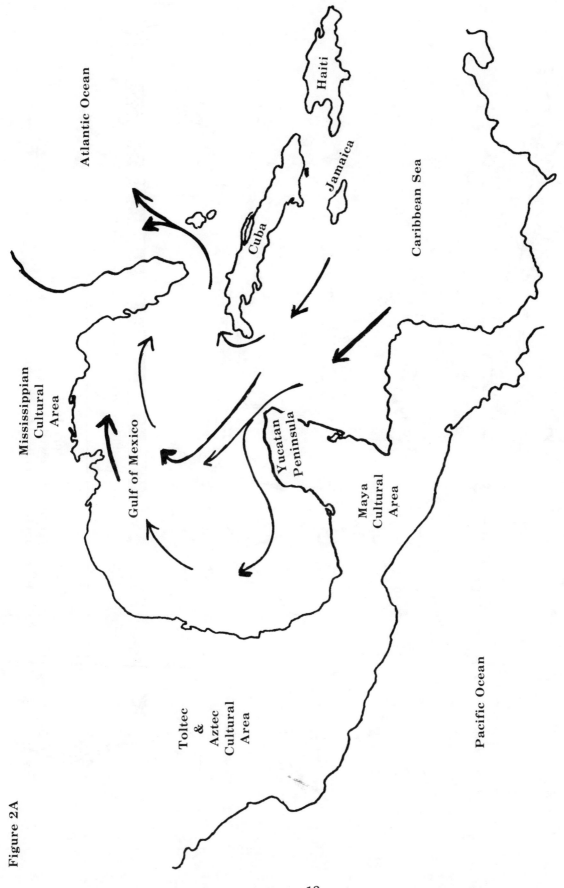

Mississippian Cultural Area

Atlantic Ocean

Haiti

Jamaica

Cuba

Caribbean Sea

Gulf of Mexico

Yucatan Peninsula

Maya Cultural Area

Toltec & Aztec Cultural Area

Pacific Ocean

Primary current past the Yucatan Peninsula and through the Gulf of Mexico.

13

Figure 3

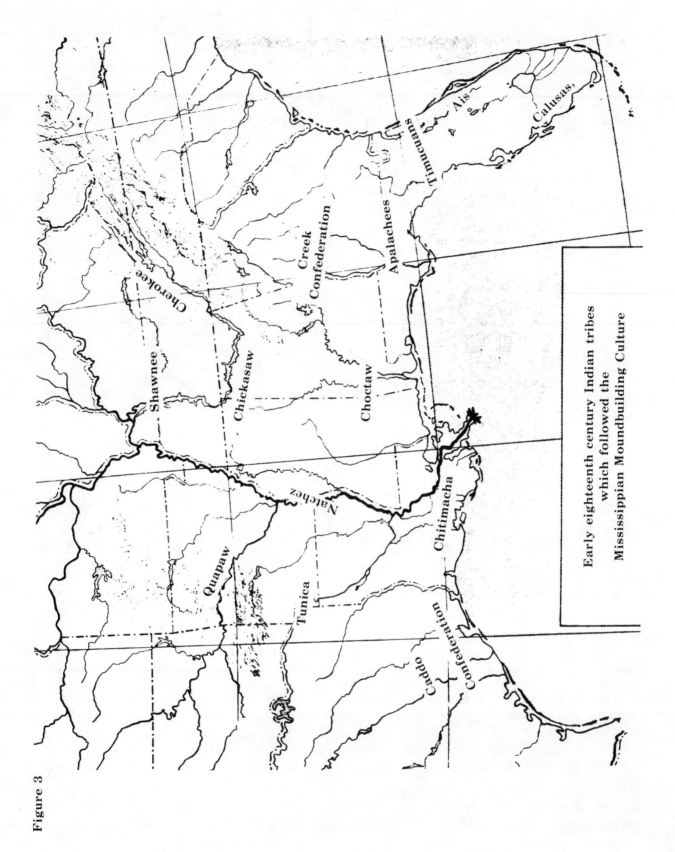

Early eighteenth century Indian tribes
which followed the
Mississippian Moundbuilding Culture

14

States we find the climate, soil and all other aspects of food gathering such that the people had time to enjoy being themselves and to develop artistic tendencies. (Figure 4 shows minimum temperatures in Florida.) The economy in the Southeast was based on agriculture with maize, squash and beans as the main crops. Many archaeologists and anthropologists say that 'the plants domesticated by the American Indians are of more commercial-industrial importance and are relied upon by more of the world's population than plants domesticated elsewhere.'[7] In addition to maize, squash and beans, the Indians who lived along the rivers, lakes and coast had a profusion of fish and seafood to subsist upon.

With this large economic base the individual families were able to gather or raise enough foodstuffs for themselves, their religious priests, their rulers, and still have enough left over for trade purposes.

Florida climate zones

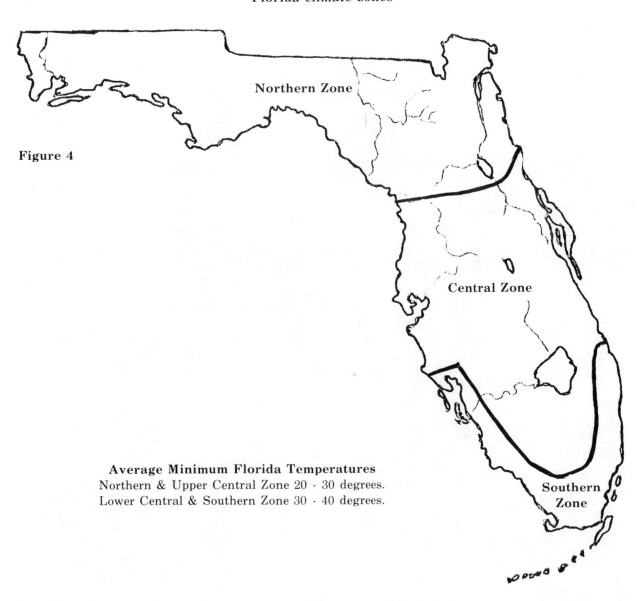

Figure 4

Average Minimum Florida Temperatures
Northern & Upper Central Zone 20 - 30 degrees.
Lower Central & Southern Zone 30 - 40 degrees.

15

The Indians in this area used a variety of tools to help in their planting and harvesting. They used large heavy hoes, weighing several pounds each, to break the soil. The blades of these hoes could be either chipped flint, shoulder blades of mammals or large bivalve shells. Shovel-like implements were used to turn the soil or to dig with. Seed was pressed into the ground with a specially made stick. They used tools of fire-hardened cane, chipped stone or metal to cut their harvest. If the land needed clearing before planting, these people used chipped stone or flint axes to clear the land. The Indians of this area did not use the 'slash and burn' agricultural method of the Central American natives

which so leeched the soil of nutrients.

To augment their agriculture, at which both men and women worked, the men hunted deer, bear, elk, bison and smaller animals. Fresh and saltwater fish and shell fish provided another important source of protein. The men were able to range all over their tribal area all year long, for game was available the entire year. The hunting of birds was not of prime importance with the exception of the turkey. The bow with small triangular arrows of chipped stone or flint was their main hunting weapon. In addition, they used deadfalls for large game and snares for small game. Fish were caught on hooks made of copper or bone attached to long fiber setlines.

Trade was carried out extensively by various segments of this culture. The hub of this trade seems to have been among the tribes occupying the northern part of Florida, all of Alabama and most of Georgia. These people had caravans or groups of artisans who would take locally grown crops or manufactured goods to different villages or tribes surrounding them. In Florida they traded for bivalve shells, alligator skins and bird plumage. They went to the tribes north of them for fresh water pearls, small shells and raw copper. To the west they traded for pottery and metal weapons. Some of the different tribes in the area mentioned acted as middlemen for flourishing trading enterprises.

Arts and Crafts

These people, unlike those tribes which lived from hand-to-mouth, were able to make items of a purely artistic nature. Approximately 90% of their pottery was for purely utilitarian purposes; the remaining 10% was for beauty and trade. The pottery for household use had no decorations although some was wrapped in a fabric made of fiber. The household pottery was usually red, brown or grey, the color showing the heating temperature of the fire and the mineral content of the clay.

The pottery made for artistic purposes and trade was made in a variety of forms. Some was painted and then glazed. Others were engraved with animal or human designs and on some, the designs were raised. Hatching and cross hatching, spirals and whorls, and geometric designs all were used, sometimes separately and at other times in combination form, to make beautiful pottery.

Another group of craftsmen worked with metal, bone and shells to make ornaments. The metal was imported from as far away as Lake Superior and was used to make tools, weapons, bracelets, headdresses, and other small items. Shells and bone were engraved and carved to form ornaments for hair and for necklaces.

Items made by this group of craftsmen, like those who made pottery, have been found in every area of the United States from the Rocky Mountains eastward and to the northern part of Mexico.

Pottery and artifacts similar to that shown in figures 5, 6, and 7 were excavated by archaeologists in the mounds around the Tampa Bay area. Since these items of fine pottery were first found in the mounds on Weeden Island in Tampa Bay, these artifacts have been identified as 'Weeden Island pottery.' This pottery shows the advanced state of the Moundbuilders Culture on the Florida Peninsula. This culture extended along the Gulf Coast north of Charlotte Harbor and somewhat inland into Mississippi,

Figure 5

Mississippian Culture bowls and bottles found at Neeley's Ferry.
A. Neeley's Ferry plain bottle with perforated base.
B. Bell plain bowls.
C. Neeley's Ferry plain bottle.
D. Neeley's Ferry bird effigy bowl.

Figure 6

Moundsville Artifacts at Alabama Museum of Natural History.

A. Ceremonial disc.   C. Incised pottery.
B. Pottery beaker or mug.   D. Incised pottery.

18

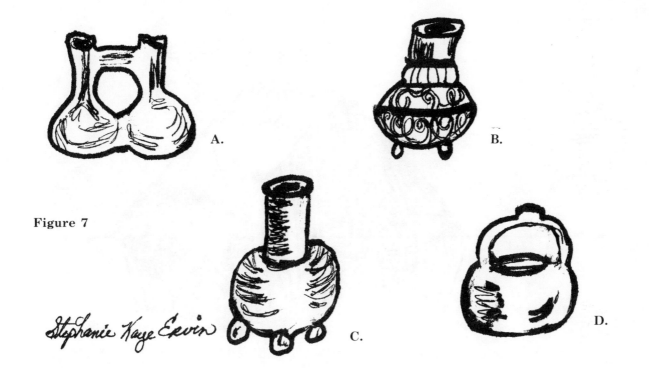

Figure 7

Stephanie Kaye Ervin

Mississippian Moundbuilder Pottery.

A. Plain double bottle.   C. Plain tripod Bottle.
B. Incised tripod Bottle.   D. Bell plain or Neeley's Ferry stirrup-necked bottle.

Alabama and southwestern Georgia. These craftsmen carved shell, bone and stone. They also used copper brought from the headwaters of the Mississippi River. They also carved quartz crystal and other stones which were brought in from the mountains. Near Pensacola they found extremely fine clay to make beautiful drinking cups and ornaments.

Architecture dealt primarily with the constructing of houses. There was no particular shape required for the houses, even though most seem to have been square or rectangular. The walls were built with wooden posts set in post holes up to 18 inches deep. Around these posts were woven flexible tree limbs or small saplings to make a sturdy wall, at times rising up to 10 feet above the ground. From the center of the dwelling four strong posts supported the roof. These four posts were approximately 48 inches apart at the base and set in a square. At the top of the roof these four posts were tied together to form the roof apex, from which saplings and small limbs were run to the side walls. Upon this framework was placed a roof of tightly woven flexible saplings. Bark or mats were added to make the roof waterproof.

A three-sided windbreak was made using the four roof supporting posts as the foundations. Within this area, the family cooking and heating fire was laid. (Figure 8.)

Religion

Religion and the trade necessary to support their religion bound the Mississippian Cultural area together.

Since they were not in fear of any lack of food, they turned their energy into religion. As has been mentioned, their

Figure 8

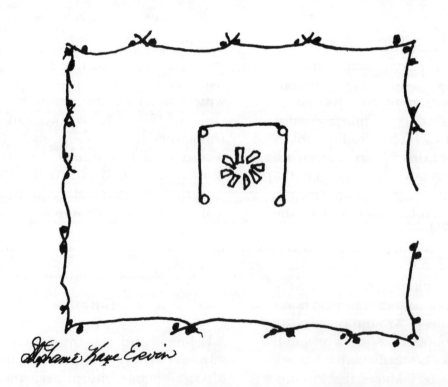

Generalized drawing of Mississippian Cultural dwelling showing side and top view.

Figure 9

'TEMPLE DES SAUVAGES'

Copied from a drawing made by French artist A De Batz when he travelled through the area in 1732-1735. Shows eagle motifs over temple.

Stephanie Kaye Ervin

Cross section of a temple mound showing construction stages.

mounds were built for the express purpose of religious worship. It was around these temples mounds that village life revolved.

The mounds usually served as the foundation for the temple or the tribal chief's house (the tribal chief was the representative of their god). These houses or temples were built of a log framework and the walls were woven of strips of tree bark. The roofs were made of tree limbs stripped of leaves and twigs. Projecting out of the center of the roof were posts with religious motifs. These houses or temples were not built to any regulated shape; some were round, others square and some rectangular in shape (figure 9).

To illustrate the enormity of the temple mounds, the one at Etowah, Georgia, is 60 feet high and the base is 330 feet by 380 feet. It has been estimated that this one mound contains 4,300,000 cubic feet of dirt, all of which was carried in large baskets on the backs of laborers. In some locations it is possible to tell, because of soil coloration, that each basket carried approximately 40-50 pounds. Each laborer got his basket of dirt from a different location than the other workers. Archaeologists also have been able to tell how the baskets were woven due to indentations in some of the soil.

When a chief or priest died, his house was razed and another level of dirt was superimposed on the original mound. In this manner, some of the mounds gradually grew until they were more than 100 feet high and covered areas up to 16 acres. (Figure 10)

The religion of this culture was centered around the feathered serpent and the sun as the primary deities. The eagle was also worshipped by these peoples and their religious year or age was 52 years in length. In these areas, worship of the serpent, sun and eagle with a 52 year religious calendar, the people show great similarity to the worship of the Mayan Culture of Central America.

Not all tribes within the Mississippian Cultural Area exhibited the bloodthirst of the Central American inhabitants.

Figure 10

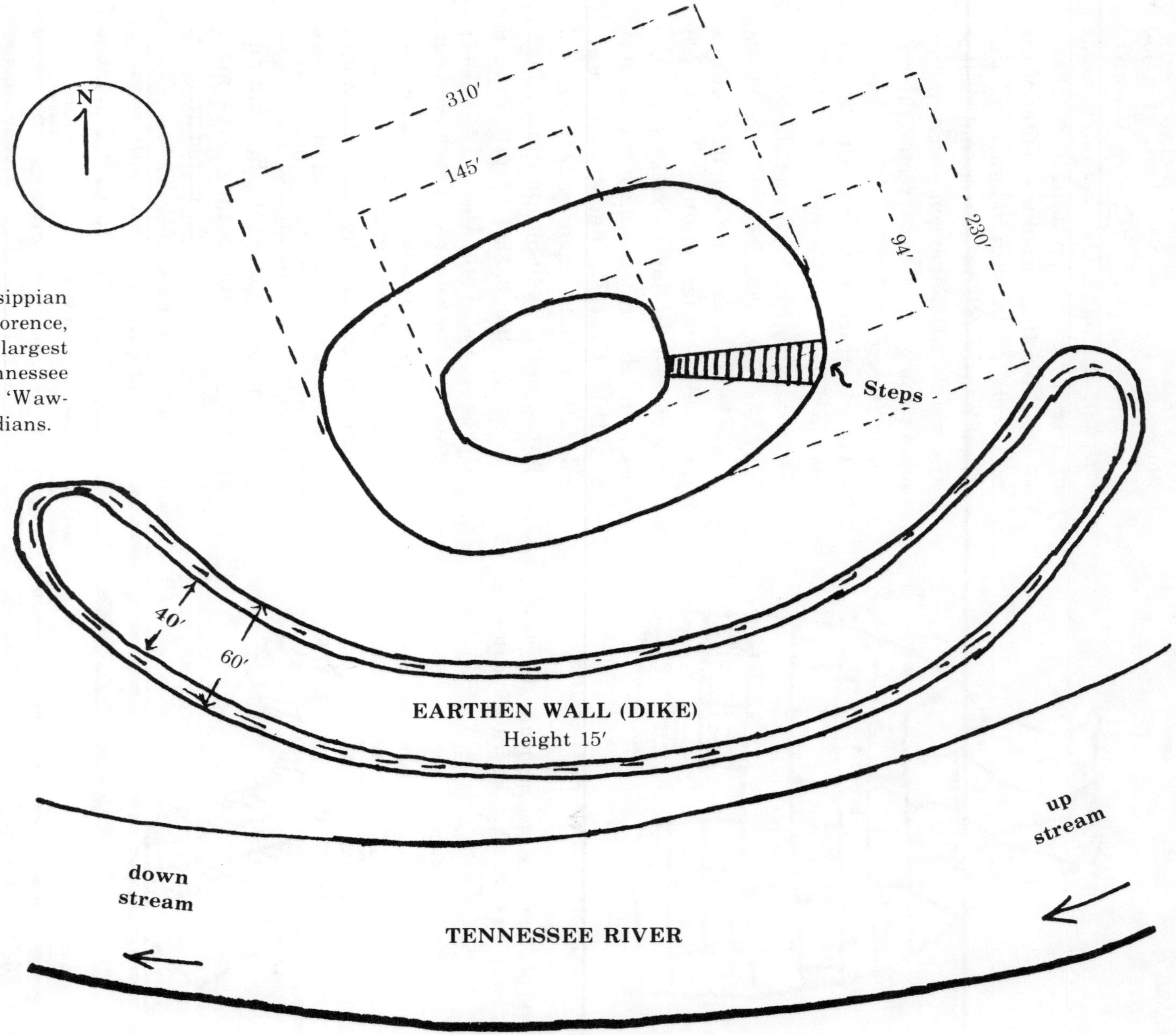

230'

94'

↰ Steps

310'

145'

Mound from Mississippian
Period located at Florence,
Ala. This is the largest
mound in the Tennessee
Valley and called 'Waw-
manona' by the Indians.

N

EARTHEN WALL (DIKE)
Height 15'

60'

40'

TENNESSEE RIVER

up
stream

down
stream

The most warlike tribes in this confederation were the Chickasaw of northern Mississippi and Alabama and the Natchez of the Mississippi River Valley area. (It is possible that the Mississippi Valley was the entrance point for any cultural diffusion from Central America. The Natchez showed more similarity to the Mayas than any other tribe in the Mississippian Moundbuilder Confederation.)

The priesthood was an important profession among this culture with the tribal ruler as the high priest. The priests carried out complex ceremonies that required years of training to learn. The arch-enemy of the priesthood was the Shaman, who taught that he had the ability to manipulate the supernatural. In that society, as in all societies, many people were superstitious, so the Shaman had many followers. The priesthood was able to negate much of the Shaman's power by giving him small official duties.

The Mississippian Moundbuilders had a clear picture of the world after death. In 1699, Lapetit, a Jesuit priest, reported:

> The rewards to which they look forward consist principally in feasting, and their chastisement in the privation of every pleasure. Thus they think that those who have been the faithful observers of their laws will be conducted into a region of pleasures, where all kinds of exquisite viands will be furnished them in abundance, that their delightful and tranquil days will flow on in the midst of festivals, dances, and women; in short, they will revel in all imaginable pleasures.[8]

But those who violated the laws or the traditions had a different sort of world to look forward to, one where they:

> . . . will be cast upon lands unfruitful and entirely covered with water, where they will not have any kind of corn, but will be exposed entirely naked to the sharp bites of mosquitos, that all Nations will make war upon them, that they will never eat meat, and have no nourishment but the flesh of crocodiles, spoiled fish, and shell-fish.[9]

Caste and Marriage

The rules regarding caste and marriage varied between the various tribes within the Mississippian Confederation.

The Natchez showed rank by tattoos and the Chickasaw painted portions of their bodies. Within the Creek Confederation, tattooing and body painting were used to denote status.

In the majority of the tribes, descent was matrilineal. One of the strangest customs regarding caste and marriage was the policies practiced by the Natchez along the Mississippi River Valley. The following description is taken from **The American Heritage Book of Indians**:

> They were ruled by a king, a descendant of the sun and called the Great Sun. Every deference was shown him, and his power over his individual subjects, their lives, labor and property, was absolute and despotic; although in political decisions involving the nation as a whole the Great Sun in turn was controlled by the council of respected old men.

His residence, in the principal village, was a large cabin (45 by 25 feet) built on a long, flat topped mound (some 8 or 10 feet high). Nearby on a similar mound was another large cabin, decorated with two carved birds perched at each end of the roof. This was the temple, in which two guardians watched the eternal fire, and in which were the sacred bones of previous Great Suns. No one but the Great Sun, who was high priest as well as king, and the few appointed temple officials, were permitted to enter the temple - whether its forbidding sanctity came primarily from the fire within it or from the bones interred there is uncertain; experts disagree.

The relatives of the Great Sun (with the exception of his children) were Little Suns: his mother or sister was the principal woman Sun and chose the successor from among her sons or brothers when the Great Sun died. The Great Sun appointed the two war chiefs of the nations, the two masters of ceremony for the public rites in the plaza before the temple, and other functionaries from among the Little Suns, all of whom were given slavish respect by the rest of the people.

Below the Suns in importance was a class of Nobles, and below the Nobles a class called Honored Men (to which anyone could aspire by distinction in war or piety), and lowest of all were the commoners, the masses, treated like dirt by the aristocrats, say the early accounts, and referred to as Stinkards, although the term was not used in the presence of the Stinkards themselves, as it offended them.

Suns could not intermarry. All Suns, male and female, including the Great Sun, had to take their wives or husbands from among the Stinkards. The children of male Suns were only Nobles, who again were obliged by law to marry Stinkards, and the children of male Nobles were reduced one more grade to Honored Men and Women, who also had to marry Stinkards. The children of Honored Men were Stinkards. Descent holding in the female line, the children of female Suns were Suns, the children of female Nobles were Nobles, the children of Honored Women were Honored People. The children of two Stinkard parents were of course absolute Stinkards.

This Gulliveresque system is unique, although its basis, descent through the mother, was and is very common among primitive societies all over the world.

Female Suns, naturally, must have held a decisive behind-the-scenes power, as well as living the life of a maiden's dream. The Stinkard husband of a woman Sun had to stand in her presence like a servant, shout his praise of her every remark, was not allowed to eat with her, and if he displeased her, particularly by any infidelity, she could 'have his head cut off in an instant.' Privilege of rank permitted her, of course, as many lovers as she pleased. She could also, if the whim struck her, have her baseborn husband thrown out at a snap of her fingers, and pick another Stinkard in his place.

During the Spanish and British Periods, from the time of Ponce de Leon's first landing on the Florida Peninsula; during the Easter season of 1514, until harmed beyond recovery by the White Man's great gifts of Pestilence, War, Famine, and Slavery, Florida was dominated by six Indian tribes or confederations. These were the Apalachees, Timucuans, Ais, Jeagas, Tekestas and Calusas. (Figure 11). These tribal names or designations could be different with different writers. For example, some writers include the Jeagas in the tribe of the Tekestas and the Ais are at times included with the Calusas. Some people also place the Jeagas and the Tekestas under the domination of the Calusas. Within 350 years of the advent of the white man on

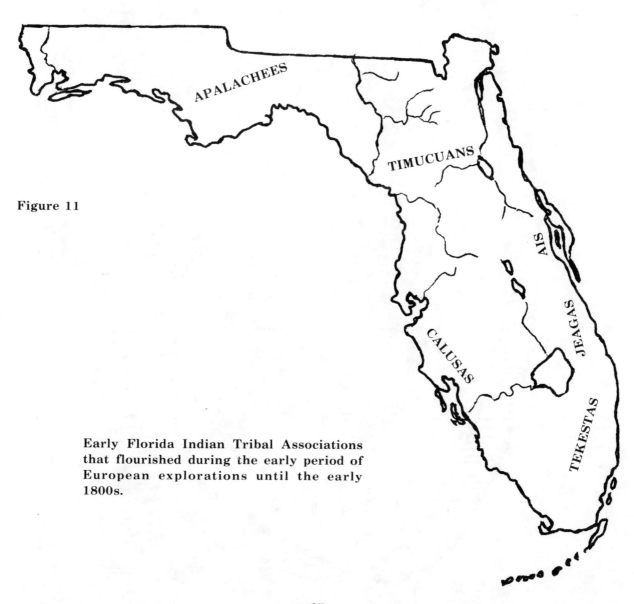

Figure 11

Early Florida Indian Tribal Associations that flourished during the early period of European explorations until the early 1800s.

Figure 12

Generalized view of Timucuan Village

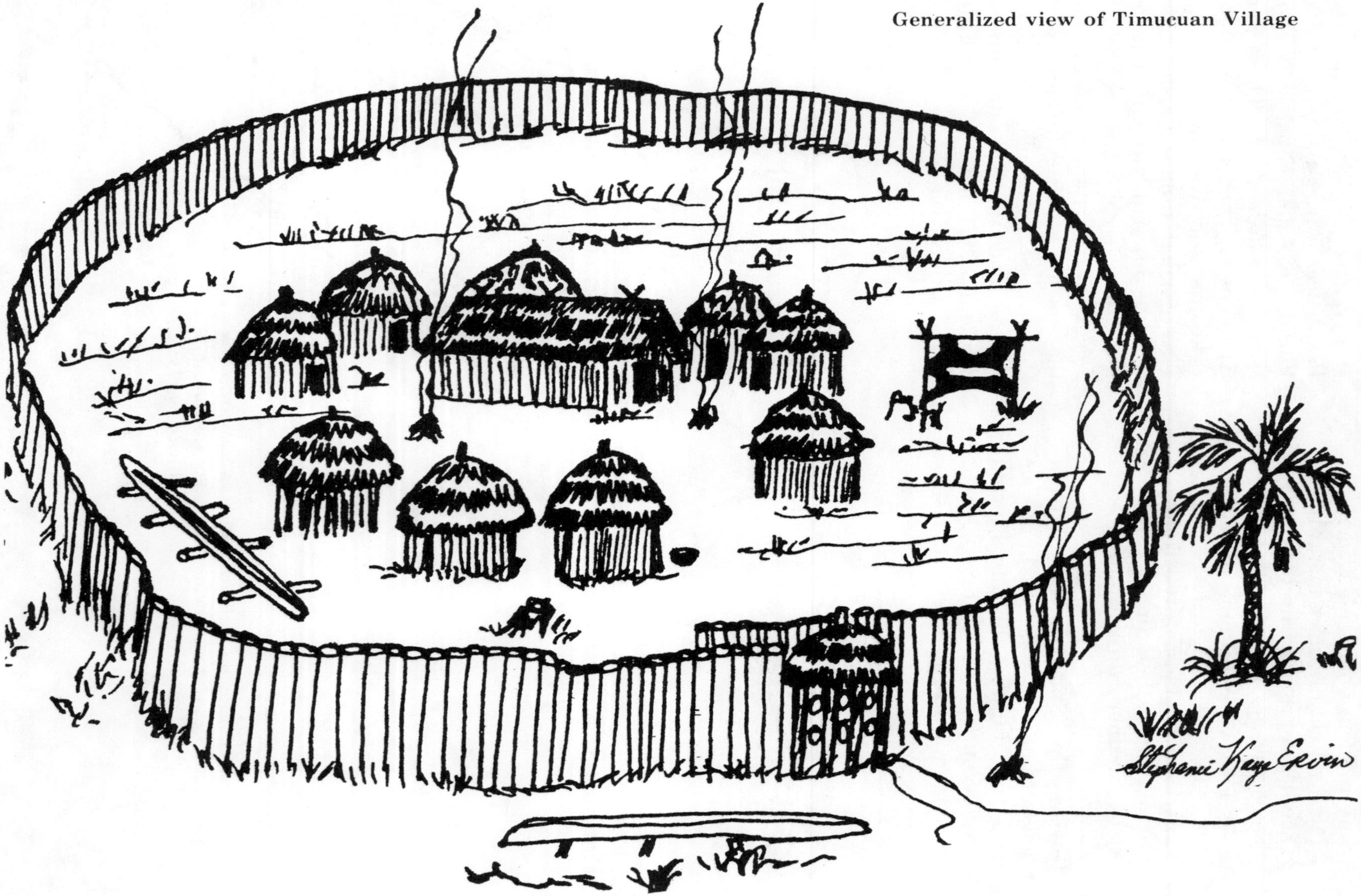

Figure 13

River Fishing

27

Figure 14

Capturing an alligator

the North American Continent, the estimated Indian population of twelve million souls in 1500 A.D. had decreased to an estimated 250,000 by 1850 A.D. It was genocide on a large scale.

The Apalachee Indians settled in the panhandle section of Florida, west of the Aucilla River. They were primarily farmers and grew crops of maize, beans, pumpkins and different types of fruit. They augmented their farming with the hunting of deer, bison, bear, and turkey. They used snares to capture quail and small game. They also spent time fishing the many lakes and streams in their area.

The Timucuans were a tribal confederation that inhabited the largest land area in Florida. Their federation ranged from the Aucilla River in the Florida panhandle south along the Gulf Coast to around the Tampa Bay area; then eastward to the Cape Canaveral area on the Atlantic Seaboard; then northward into south Georgia; from there west to the Aucilla River. They, like the Apalachees, had subsistence farming with their main crops being maize, beans, tubers and a few vegetables. They also had various kinds of fruit. The men hunted deer, bison, alligator, bear, and trapped small game. This tribe, with the Apalachees and the Calusas (to a lesser degree), were members of the Mississippian Moundbuilder Culture. The mounds at Fort Walton Beach are a notable example of their work. Lesser mounds are spotted all over central and north Florida.

Just south of the Timucuans lived the Ais. They resided from the Cape Canaveral area south to the St. Lucie River inlet. Their range was east of this river to the Atlantic Ocean. This tribe was primarily food gatherers from the abundant natural vegetation of the area.

They subsisted on palm berries, coco plums and sea grapes plus a variety of fish and shellfish. The Ais did not develop the village system of either the Timucuans or the Apalachees. This lack of a village system could be attributed to the type of food gathering subsistence of these people. They were quite warlike and some writers say that it was the Ais that Ponce de Leon had a battle with when he first landed in Florida. According to the journal of Jonathan Dickinson this Tribal Confederation's influence over them was stronger than the Jeagas just south of them. Dickinson mentions the fact that one of the chiefs of the Ais, hearing that a chief of the Jeagas had taken gold and silver from Dickinson's party, organized a party to get a share of this money.

The Jeagas resided south of the Ais near present Palm Beach. Very little is known of them but Jonathan Dickinson (who was shipwrecked on their coast in 1696) said they seemed to be cannibals. It is also reported that the Ais and the Jeagas plundered wrecked ships and placed any gold and silver found in pits in the ground. Dickinson also reported that his party used the Spanish language with the Indians along the east coast of Florida so that they would obtain more favorable treatment. It seems that the Indian tribes in the east of Florida disliked the English very much and would kill any English found.

The Tekestas ranged south of the Jeagas to the Florida Keys. They subsisted primarily by fishing and gathering sea grapes or coco plums. It is reported that they preserved and worshipped two bones which they extracted from the head of any manatee they killed. These tribes, the Tekestas, and the Jeagas, seem to be the most primitive of the Florida Indian tribes. In the mid-sixteenth century, the Jesuits established a mission on the site of present Miami to attempt to Christ-ianize these people. This mission lasted only a few years before it withdrew to St. Augustine. Some writers and historians feel that the Tekestas and the Jeagas are branches of the same tribe. There is no information regarding the Jeagas in the seventeenth century in Spanish sources; the only information is from Jonathan Dickinson's journal.

The descriptions which we have of the houses of the Southeastern Coastal Indians (Jeagas and Tekestas) show them to be of simple tepee design. They were constructed of four saplings shoved into the ground and then tied together with a vine near the apex. Palmetto leaves or palm branches were used as a covering. These weakly constructed houses were usually destroyed during any heavy rain or wind storm. This type of house construction also showed the nomadic existence these tribes had in their hand-to-mouth food gathering livelihood.

The Calusas had an estimated fifty villages between the Lake Okeechobee area and Tampa Bay. This tribal confederation was quite warlike and exacted tribute from the Tekestas south of them. By conquest and the exacting of tribute the Calusas organized all south Florida tribes into a semi-peaceful federation. They carried out extensive trade within their confederation. In 1545, this tribe captured a 15 year old Spanish lad named Domingo Escalante de Fontaneda. Years later he was rescued by a Spanish exploration party and returned to Spain. There he wrote the first book about Florida, describing in detail the culture of his Indian captors.

The clothing of many of the Florida Indians was quite simple. The women wore skirts made of moss. The clothing for the men was a triangular piece of reed or fiber material woven or plaited together. From the top two points a woven band of this material, (approximately) four fingers wide, extended for tying at the person's back. From the third point of the triangle another narrow piece of material extended. To a European observer this piece at the man's back resembled a small horse tail. For colder weather they used animal hides to break some of the wind and rain.

During the early part of the eighteenth century, Florida experienced a peaceful invasion along the north central boundary. This invasion came from roving bands of Muskogee, Hitchiti and remnants of other tribes of the Creek Confederation. As members of the Mississippi Culture these tribes had been involved in trade with their southern neighbors. The area these Creeks moved into had formerly been occupied by the Apalachee Tribe. The Apalachees had lost some of their population by disease brought by the white man and some by inter-tribal warfare. They could have recovered from this, but in 1704 an event occurred which destroyed completely this indian nation. Governor Moore of South Carolina, with a large group of Creek allies, invaded Apalachee territory and began a war of extermination. The Apalachees and all other Florida tribes, except the Calusas, were allied with Spain. Spain and England were at war at this time, with both sides making raids into their enemies' territory. During 1704-1705, the British were able to utterly destroy the Apalachee Nation. The Apalachees who were not killed were sold into slavery. With the elimination of this tribe a void was left in north central Florida. This void was soon filled by Muskogee and Hitchiti

Creeks. The Hitchiti Creeks were a determined and resolute tribe - one of the most warlike in the Creek Confederation. It was from this branch of the Creeks that a most important ingredient entered into the Seminole Confederation. That ingredient was determination.

The name these Indians bore was Isti-se-mo-le. Many definitions have been given for this name; among them are wanderer, separatist, outcast, runaway, and immigrant. Colonel Benjamin Hawkins, appointed by the United States goverment in 1785 to negotiate a treaty with the Creeks, states that the name means wild man. As he was for many years the Indian agent in Georgia and the Mississippi Territory, living among the people, it is safe to assume that his definition is fairly accurate.

During the eighteenth century the English, with their Creek allies, made many raids into Spanish territory and slowly destroyed the Indian allies of Spain. As Spain was slowly weakening as a power, she found it increasingly difficult to afford her Indian allies any protection. Due to this lack of Spanish aid the Apalachees were destroyed as a nation by 1705. In the next seventy years the Timucuans, Calusas and the wilder tribes along the southeastern seaboard had almost been exterminated by warfare and disease brought by the white man. The few remaining members of the early Indian tribes either retreated into the fastness of the Everglades or were absorbed into the in-migration of the Seminoles.

The Seminole Confederation was allowed to settle peacefully and unmolested by the Spanish government throughout Florida. The Seminoles settled in well built villages. Some of these Indians became farmers, raising a variety of crops, while others became ranchers with herds of cattle. The Seminoles seem to have assimilated all the best parts of the various cultures they came in contact with, but with little warlike tendencies until provoked. They welcomed the Negro who was fleeing from slavery in Georgia and the Mississippi Territory; they also welcomed any Creeks or Cherokees who fled from white oppression. The Negroes seemed to have been placed in a vassal state within the Seminole Confederation. Even though many rose to positions of great authority, they still were in a very loose slave (or vassal) state. That is, though they enjoyed quite a large amount of freedom, they were obliged to give the Indians a token payment of corn or cattle or some other item each year.

While Spain controlled Florida the Indians were citizens of Spain. In 1763, when Florida was transferred from Spanish rule to English, the few early Indians remaining (Timucuans, Calusas, Apalachee and others) left Florida for Cuba and other Spanish controlled islands. The Seminoles remained in Florida and became faithful British subjects. From this time, 1763, until the Americans invaded Spanish Florida in 1819, the Seminoles looked to England for assistance and advice. Even though Florida reverted to Spain in 1783, it was England who controlled the Seminole Confederation. During the American Revolution many of the Georgia Creeks and Florida Seminoles assisted the British military forces in raids in the Carolinas and Georgia. Many of the Southern whites never forgave the Indians for the assistance they gave England. Because of this long seated dislike, any time there was any border infraction it was always the Indian who was at fault. Yet once the revolution was over the Seminoles returned to their homes and villages and took up their peaceful pursuits of farming and ranching. To show the peaceful nature of the Seminoles after the revolution, Reverend Jebidiah Morse, appointed as a commissioner to investigate Indian conditions in 1820, had this to say:

> Before the wars of 1812, and since, these Indians with their Negro slaves, lived in comfort, and many of them were wealthy in cattle and horses.[10]

It is only in a peaceful environment that these Indians could have become wealthy in cattle and horses.

FOOTNOTES

[1] Capt. Mayne Reid, **Osceloa the Seminole**.
[2] Diary of Dr. M. S. Jarvis, p. 13.
[3] Ibid., p. 16.
[4] Ibid., p. 25.
[5] Paul Eugene Camp, **Boredom, Brandy & Bickering**.
[6] Farb, **Man's Rise to Civilization**.
[7] Jennings, **Prehistory in North America**.
[8] Farb.
[9] Farb.
[10] Coe, Charles H., **Red Patriots**, p. 9.

SETTLERS

To the first white settlers, America seemed a paradise, a land of boundless plenty where the skies were darkened by flocks of birds, where the rivers brimmed with fish, and the fertile earth was veined with precious ores. But, rich though it may have been in natural resources, this land was poor in people. The scattered bands of red men fought the whites, fled, or died; the boundless forests of oak and beech and elm lay silent and deserted. The settler sought fortunes from the production and export of commercial crops - rice, sugar, tobacco, wheat, and rum; these fortunes might not be made unless there was ample labor available to clear the trees, plant the land, cultivate the crops, and harvest them.

The Ballad of America

THE WORKERS

Woodrow Wilson, when president of Princeton University, made the remark that a student could learn the history of any nation just by studying the lives of its notable citizens. The same could be said of a study of the history of Florida - just study the lives of De Soto, Reid, Gamble, Ormond, Anderson, Bulow, Perpal, Hernandez, Pellicer, and all the other well known explorers and settlers and you will learn the history of this state. But Florida was not really built and settled by the notable citizens - it was built by the blood, sweat and tears of the slaves and the yeomen farmers. It does not matter whether the slaves were the Indians who built the Castillo de San Marcos and other Spanish enclaves, or the indentured servants of Turnbull who constructed New Smyrna and other early British plantation systems, or the blacks who were stuffed five and six hundred together in the holds of the slave ships and sent to the new world to build the economic base of the large and small plantations for the Americans, or the convicts on chain gangs who constructed and maintained so many of the roads, railways and drainage systems in this state. Chains are chains whether they are made of iron or of velvet. It was the slaves and the indentured servants and the yeomen farmers who supplied the manpower to build Florida. Without this mass of humanity which came either voluntarily or involuntarily, the few free wealthy citizens of the territory could not have accomplished much and in many cases could not have survived.

During the nineteenth century the living conditions among all the middle and low income groups in the United States were nearly identical. Food, clothing, housing, medical care and entertainment available to both free and slave were virtually the same. In many cases the food, clothing and medical resources available to the slave were vastly superior to these same items offered to the free. In one aspect only were those free superior to the slave, and this was the most important part of a person's being: Their ability to move anywhere, anytime and perform any job they wanted to and were qualified to do. Included in this was the possibility of reaching top level management positions if they were qualified.

Many of the Europeans who came to the Floridas did not have enough money to pay their passage. To compensate for this and so that they could get a fresh start in a land rich in natural resources, or possibly to escape from uncomfortable circumstances, people would sell their services to a wealthy patron, or company, that owned land in the new world. The person would sign a contract of indenture, promising to do servitude for a specified number of years, usually from three to seven. The patron would guarantee food, clothing, housing, medical care, time off and other needs for the life of the contract. Once the term of service was completed the indentured servants were freed to go anywhere they wanted and to do as they pleased. Also, if the contract so specified, they might receive a complete set of new clothing, weapons and possibly a small section of land.

Turnbulls' Indentured Servants

Many indentured servants, apprentice laborers and journeymen were required to work six days a week and from twelve to sixteen hours per day and they had to prepare their own food. Slaves were frequently worked much less than this except during the busy times of the year (planting and harvesting times and then only during hours of daylight). The indentured servants and apprentices had little or no recourse to the legal system of that time. The master could do as he wished to the worker, almost as far as taking the person's life. This is shown with regard to the indentured servants Dr. Turnbull, in 1768, brought into Florida from the Mediterranean area (most came from the island of Minorca). Their indenture contract called for three years service in return for transportation to the Americas, housing, clothing, food and other necessities. Turnbull, for some reason, did not plan the project properly and signed up more servants than the project could use and so was unable to keep his part of the contract. The food was poor, clothing minimal, housing not sufficient for the amount of people and other failings. At the end of the three year contract Turnbull and his overseers enslaved the indentured servants and forced them into another four years of servitude. During this extra four year period the Minorcans rebelled against the harsh treatment and enslavement. The revolt was put down with the aid of British soldiers and the leaders were executed. Soon after this Dr. Turnbull became embroiled in a political dispute with the British governor, Tonyn. In early 1777 a group of Minorcans, led by a carpenter named Pellicer, requested from the overseer permission to go fishing so they could supplement the food supply. As the authorities in New Smyrna did not know of the real destination of Pellicer and his group, permission was granted. As soon as they were out of sight of land the group began their seventy odd mile trip to St. Augustine. The Minorcans saw Governor Tonyn and placed their list of grievances before him. The governor agreed that the indentured servants had been ill-used and ordered them freed from bondage. He also gave Pellicer a safe conduct to New Smyrna so that Turnbulls' overseers could be informed of the turn of events. Governor Tonyn asked that the Minorcans and the other freed servants return to St. Augustine. This they did in early 1777 and were resettled in the northern sector of the town. The descendants of these indentured servants are leading citizens of St. Augustine today.

Indentured servants were often treated less humanely than slaves. This was because those who were indentured would be freed from their contract within a relatively short time, whereas a slave would always remain the owner's valuable property until he was sold or died.

Slave Trade

The sugar and indigo industry in East Florida required a large work force. As there was not an ample supply of voluntary labor, it was necessary that involuntary labor be obtained. This involuntary work force was at first captured Indians, but as they were not suitable for forced labor they were quickly replaced by African blacks. Most blacks who came to this country did not come of their own free will, as the indentured servants did, nor did they have much hope of working off their servitude. Most blacks had been captured in Africa by Moslem slave traders or by other African tribesmen who then sold them to the Moslems. The slave traders moved their human cargo to an African port city and there sold the captives to ship masters. In 1861 the average price for a human at an African port was fifty dollars. Once transported across the Atlantic Ocean and sold in Cuba, the average price asked was seventy-eight dollars. In 1853 the general prices asked in Richmond, Virginia, for slaves were: Best men (18-25) $1200 to $1300; fair men (18-25) $959 to $1050; boys (five feet in height) $850 to $950; young women $800 to $1000. Remember that these prices were paid in the mid nineteenth century when the average worker in the United States made less than eight hundred dollars a year. According to some economists, the price paid for slaves by the American plantation owner was tied into the price for which cotton sold. If a pound of cotton sold for twelve cents, then the asking price for an average field hand would be twelve hundred dollars. Those who were artisans or semi-skilled or with managerial abilities, and this constituted around 25 percent of the slave force, commanded much higher prices.

Slaves bound for the new world would have a stop-over in the Caribbean area, possibly in Cuba or the West Indies. Those slaves destined for the United States resumed their unwanted trip and landed in some port city, possibly Charleston, Savannah or New Orleans. Once at their destination they were forced in chains off the vessel. After spending some time in temporary quarters (salve pens) where they could regain some composure, the slaves were sold at public auction. After purchase, the slave dealer usually drove his 'marketable goods' in coffles to other areas for resale. A coffle is what a slave train is called - the males manacled and chained in pairs, the females and children walking along with them. The coffle was always accompanied by supply wagons, in which any women or children who passed out or were unable to keep up could be placed, one or two

fiddlers and the slave traders. The fiddlers played lively tunes to create an atmosphere of happiness among the slaves. The fiddlers were usually owned by the slave traders and were well cared for.

Once the slave caravan reached a market town the slaves were placed in slave pens where they were groomed for the forthcoming sale. The proposed sale was well advertised so that many people would attend. To be groomed for the sale the slaves were well fed, given clean clothes and rested. On the day of the sale they could be given a large drink of whiskey to make them appear more frisky. Once sold to plantation owners, the slaves were moved to their home for the next years. One point of interest is that as early as 1700 the majority of slaves in the American colonies were native born and by 1800 less than 20 percent were African born. This means that most slaves were at least second generation Americans by 1800 and many were fourth generation Americans. In the Caribbean and South America the death rate among the slaves was so high they needed constant replacements and so the majority were African born.

There were two generalized classifications or groups of slaves - those who were city dwellers and those who were rural. The slaves who lived in the city, as a rule, had more freedom than those located on the plantations. About six percent of the slaves were employed in urban areas and their occupations were classed as skilled or semi-skilled. This means they were carpenters, house servants, millers, blacksmiths, brick masons, etc. The urban slave was frequently allowed to hire out his or her services to anyone who wanted or needed his services. The owner had to know who was doing the hiring, how much was being paid (often a contract was drawn up between the owner and the renter stipulating all aspects of the transaction), what the task would be, how long the task should take and what portion of the rental monies the owner would receive and what the slave would receive. From the monies received for this hiring out process, the slave could eventually save enough money to buy his freedom or, if the worker wanted to, he could purchase some item that would please him.

Somewhere around the mid 1850s, more stringent slave laws were voted into effect in the different southern states. Most of these laws came into effect because of the violent policies of the abolitionists, the refusal of many northern states to abide by the laws of the United States and by the aborted insurrection led by John Brown. Normally, when there was fear of a slave uprising the local militia instituted strong slave patrols.

Slaves on plantations were treated somewhat differently than those in cities. Their free time was much more closely supervised, and during slack times they could be rented out to work for someone else. The slaves were seldom able to retain any of the money they earned from their labors. It was also possible that the person who contracted for their services would give them less than adequate care - working them longer hours than their owner would, less favorable medical care, poor housing and food, and even stricter supervision.

Working Hours

The hours worked varied with the seasons of the year, type of labor performed (whether artisan, semi-skilled, or laborer), if agricultural - the cash crop under cultivation and the disposition of the owner of the plantation. In Florida some plantation owners had their field hands out from sun-up till late afternoon. They could have breakfast in the fields or at their quarters and then start the day's labor. Lunch could also be in the field and would last anywhere from one to three hours, depending on the season. After the noon break, the day's work would be finished and the slaves returned to their quarters. During the day, it was normal for the slaves to take a water or rest break when they needed it as long as the break was not abused.

Most plantations had a kitchen staff which prepared meals for the work force. This was because often the field hands were too tired to prepare their own meals properly, or even to prepare one at all. In addition, the centralised meal preparations meant that the slaves could spend more time working, and thus could be more productive for their owners. After returning from the fields, usually a few hours before sunset, the slaves were free to use the time as they pleased. This could be working in their own garden, strolling by themselves or with their mates, fishing to augment their diet and generally taking things easy. Once the day's work was finished, it was normal for the owner to inspect the work done during the day, talking with the foreman about the day's work and then issuing instructions for the following day.

It was usual for the slaves to have one-half day Saturday and all day Sunday off. The reason for the half work day on Saturday was for cleanliness of the slaves. This day was spent in bathing, washing clothes, cleaning around the cabins and general cleaning work.

House Servants

The house servants were under much

less supervision than the field workers. They were often treated as members of the family and frequently acted that way. Their duties and hours were much more flexible than the field hands', their food and clothing was equal to that of the owner's family. However, not all house slaves were well treated. The disposition of the owner or the spouse had quite a bit to do with the slave's treatment. Two free blacks, Charles and Anna Dorsey of Maryland, were kidnapped by a professional 'nigger trader.' The kidnapper would tie his vessel at some port or landing, then he and his cronies would roam the countryside capturing any black they could find. It did not matter if the black was slave or free - as long as they were black they were free game to be sold into slavery again and in an area far away from where they were captured. The Dorseys, captured by this slave trader, were transported to Florida and there sold to a Colonel Louis Matair of Suwannee County.

Colonel Matair was a very kind individual. However his wife was the opposite - a cruel and vindictive person. Once on the plantation, the Dorseys were assigned to their tasks - she became a house-maid while he became a mechanic (when free this was his livelihood in Maryland). To illustrate Mrs. Matairs' cruelty, witnesses reported that she would personally whip any slave she considered impertinent. Once Mrs. Matair called out to Anna Dorsey - Anna, not hearing, continued her duties. Mrs. Matair burst into an angry frenzy and entered the room where Anna was working and, seizing a butcher knife, slashed at Anna. In warding off the blow Anna received a gash on her arm which incapacitated her for quite a while. This was not the normal treatment accorded the slaves.

Many were treated with extreme kindness according to the standards of the time.

Food

The usual recorded rations for slaves were pork, corn and sweet potatoes. For this reason some people believe that this constituted the slaves' entire or primary diet, however these items were recorded because they constituted elements of the diet that could be stored for the entire year. Most fruit and vegetables were available only during certain seasons of the year and were quite difficult or impossible to store. Also rations which were easily available on a year round basis did not enter in any of the overseer's instructions. For example, along the Halifax and Hillsboro Rivers of East Florida, the fish and shellfish were so plentiful that there was no need to mention them in the lists of instructions of food supplied to the slaves. Even up to the 1950s, blue crabs with shells of 18-24 inches were available in the Daytona Beach area of the Halifax River; also oysters, mullet and other fish were so plentiful it was normal to bring them home by the basketfull. The plantations in East Florida had ample supplies of beef, fowl, citrus fruits, sugar, molasses, rice, corn, squash, beans, wild game and other food-stuffs grown in this climate.

Housing

As Florida was a frontier territory, the housing for the gentry, the free workers, and the slave workers was not of the quality of housing found in other parts of the South. The mounds on which the slave cabins of the Addison Plantation stood (Tomoka River area) now measure approximately 20 feet by 20 feet. As the plantation was constructed during the

Typical slave or tenant cabin as reproduced at the Pike Pioneer Museum, Troy, Alabama.

Typical log cabin as used by a plantation owner, overseer, or farm family during the early to mid 1800s. Reproduced at the Pike Pioneer Museum, Troy, Alabama.

early part of the nineteenth century, it is quite possible that these building mounds could easily have been 28 feet by 28 feet. This would give an approximate dimension to the cabin of 24 feet by 24 feet with an inside floor space in excess of 550 square feet. This was a good size cabin at that time.

According to census information, from 1860, the average number of slaves for each of the slave quarters on large plantations was 5.2, whereas there was an average of 5.3 persons in the households of the free workers. The sharing of common quarters or communal style living was very unusual among both the slave and the free families during the 1800s. One weak point in the 1860 housing census report was that it did not contain any information on the size or quality of the housing occupied. The descriptions in plantation records and in travellers' commentaries is quite fragmented and varied. They show a very large range in size and in quality - from three or four room cottages of wood, brick or stone construction, having up to eight hundred feet of living space with large porches, fireplaces, and glazed windows down to single room log cabins with floors of earth, or possibly wooden planks lying directly on the earth. Of course, there would be a fireplace for heating and cooking. As many of the fireplace chimneys were constructed of mud and sticks, they often caught fire and would burn the cabin. By the housing standards of the 1980s, the housing for the slaves and free workers was very inadequate. By the standards of the early 1800s, the housing was quite spacious. In 1893 a housing survey in 'New York City revealed that the median number of square feet of sleeping space per person was just 35.' It is quite possible that the typical slave quarters of the early nineteenth century had more sleeping space available per person than the typical living quarters that the workers in New York City had in the later part of the century.

Medical

It was usual for each plantation to have either hospital or medical facilities available to all those who lived on it. The hospital could range in size from a small one room log cabin up to a two story frame house. The larger facilities contained separate rooms for different medical purposes. One room would be for maternity purposes, another for those with need for confinement and a special room would be available for outpatient treatment. At times the plantation owner would set aside several rooms in his home for medical purposes. More frequently the plantation medical facility would be a two sectioned log or frame house with each section having two or three rooms. No matter what type of facility was available, the men and women were kept separate. Few plantations retained a full time physician, but almost all of them had a full time nurse. This nurse, usually an elderly slave, had under her authority several midwives. The nurse, and doctor if available, not only treated the slaves but all the residents of the plantations. She worked under the direct authority of the owner or overseer. These individuals had to keep abreast of all the latest medical information available and this information was quite primitive by any standard. It was usual for most diseases to be treated in a way that would be harmful to the patient. For example: it was believed that most disease was caused by 'poisons emanating from decaying animal and vegetable matter.' These poisons entered the body by drinking impure water or by breathing

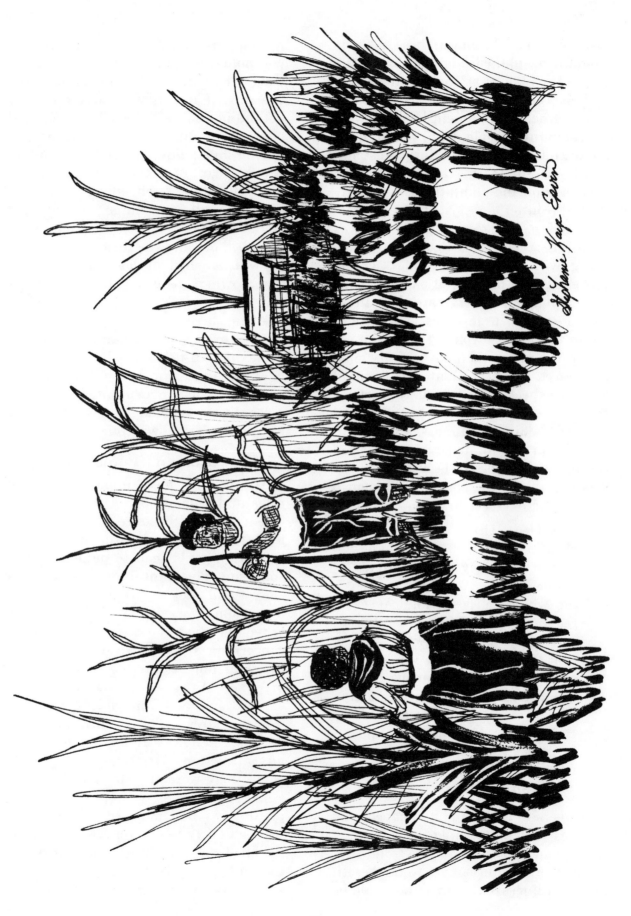

stale air. To eliminate these poisons from the body, the leading doctors of the day advocated that their patients (or victims) be bled, blistered or purged. This method of treatment hurried to the grave many people who would have regained their health if allowed rest and fluids. Frequently, the nurses and overseers on the plantations, especially in the frontier areas such as Florida, administered folk medicines, such as herbs, to their sick. Because of this, along with less reliance on bleeding, blistering and purging of patients, they had a higher recovery rate than those who lived in large cities. The theory regarding disease coming from impure water or bad air did have one very good side effect. It led the planters to demand and to expect good hygienic practices from all their workers. They expected personal bodily cleanliness, all clothing to be clean and all items in and around the living quarters to be kept clean. It was normal for the plantation owner to require the overseer to

> see that they keep their clothing mended and clean, and that they wash their clothes as often as once a week, for which purpose time must regularly be set apart at the end of the week. He must see that they are clean on Sundays and not straggling about the country dirty and ragged, and he must see that they appear clean every Monday morning in the year, without any failure whatever (Fogel & Engerman: **Time on the Cross**).

The overseer also had to inspect the living quarters to make certain they were clean and the yard free from filth. If the overseer did not see to the health and cleanliness of the slaves he would be judged 'unfit for the responsible station you hold' and immediately discharged. Once discharged for this offense the overseer, if free, would have difficulty obtaining another job in the area and if a slave, would find life intolerable among his fellow workers. To aid in slaves' cleanliness, the plantation owner required that each slave cabin be emptied of all furnishings (so they could be aired out), the interior completely scrubbed out and the inside and outside be whitewashed at least once a year. Some owners required this up to three times a year. Many owners also required that the slave cabins be relocated every two or three years for sanitary reasons. Time allowed to do this house cleaning or painting and the relocating of quarters was incorporated into the normal work schedule and was not done on the workers' own time.

Rewards and Punishments

All societies have imposed a set of rules and regulations on their subjects. Obedience to these regulations could lead to favorable treatment and any infraction could lead to punishment of some sort. The plantation owners used a 'carrot and stick' approach to obtaining maximum work from their laborers. When we read the various state laws concerning slavery, we often feel that the punishment was too severe for the offense. Many of these laws were enacted in haste and during times of internal stress. They called for slave patrols and quite strict punishments for any infractions. (It seems strange that when there were any slave uprisings so very few slaves joined them. Few plantations had more than five or six whites to fifty to two hundred blacks. If the blacks were so ill-treated, why didn't they all rise up in rebellion when there were slave uprisings? Nat Turner, in

Tidewater, Virginia, received few recruits in his rebellion and John Brown received no recruits. In fact, blacks played an important part in putting down slave rebellions many times.) The slave patrols covered a specific area or district each night and if someone, white or black, was found roaming around the countryside without good reason, that person would be questioned on the spot or brought before a justice of the peace for questioning. Too frequently, some of the slave patrols took their assignment too seriously and slaves were jailed and beaten for no reason. White or black, slave or free, all were subjected to being interrogated, beaten and jailed for being out after curfew - but the black was more liable to be classified as a troublemaker if he was not known, and friendly toward someone on the patrol. During the Spanish and British periods in St. Augustine the military patrolled the city streets after curfew at night. If someone was found out of doors after curfew, that individual was liable to be shot as a possible robber.

It is often hard for us to understand that in the South there were two sets of laws for the slaves - one was the state law, which was often quite severe, and the other was the law of the plantation, which was often quite liberal and fair. It was the law of the plantation to which the slave adhered. We have the same situation today in many of our college or university towns, in state and federal government and in many other areas of our daily lives. For example, the federal government enacts speed laws for vehicular traffic on national highways. Once that highway enters a different state, the speed limit could be changed to conform to that state's laws. Also, colleges and universities frequently have regulations which are different from state or federal laws - yet the student must obey the school rules to remain in good standing. We all recognize this today and the slave had the same thing to contend with - and the law of the plantation was supreme.

Slavery did exploit those who were in bondage and this was quite readily seen in the rewards and punishments given out. Punishment could consist of whippings (and this was the most common punishment), being deprived of privileges (going to town, fishing, recreation, or other small amenities of life), confinement in stocks, exportation (to another state or foreign nation), sale in the local area, branding or the death penalty. It was usual when the death penalty was administered to a slave, for the penalty to be changed to a severe whipping and then re-sale for exportation to another state or a foreign nation. By this changing of the sentence the owner was able to realize some monetary return from the slave.

Whipping is thought by many people to have been the primary method of work motivation among the slaves. Yet whipping could not motivate anyone into performing their best. Some of the most reliable data concerning the frequency of whipping is found in the diary of Bennet Barrow of Louisiana. He had around 120 slaves in his work force. In a two year period, 1840-42, he records a total of 160 whippings administered with more than half his workers receiving no punishment whatsoever. Beating of workers was more prevalent in the South than the North because of the economic situation. In the North, workers who were lazy or in any way shirked their duties could be fired and thus left to starve out of the eyesight of the employer. Curtailing of food was seldom used to discipline slaves: Lack of adequate food would hurt the productivity of the slave.

43

Planters motivated their workers through systems of rewards and praise. Rewards could be short term: The individual or gang having the best picking, harvesting or planting record for a given day or week might get extra clothing, tobacco, whiskey, cash, or even an unscheduled holiday or trip to town.

If slaves worked on their normal days off, they usually received the prevailing area wage for their work. Slaves who were performing above average were allowed to work on their off duty time making items to sell in the neighborhood. Cash received for items sold in this manner belonged exclusively to the slave. At the year's end, slaves were also given a bonus for work well done. On some plantations, slaves could earn in excess of one hundred dollars per year. If these 1840 dollars were translated into 1980 dollars, slaves could earn in excess of eight thousand dollars a year.

There were also rewards of a long term nature. The slaves could rise in the social and economic atmosphere of bondage. Field hands had the opportunity to become artisans or drivers. These artisans had the opportunity to move from plantation to plantation and to hire themselves out. The driver could become the head driver and then the overseer. Advancing along the economic ladder brought social status, more freedom, better housing, better clothing, and more cash. Prior to the vehemence caused by the abolitionists in the 1850s, a good number of slaves were able to purchase their freedom under the work incentive program of the planters.

Re-sale

Writers and historians sometimes mention 'slave breeding farms' and the sale of any offspring. These probably did not exist. The cost of raising a child to around ten years of age, the lack of productive labor from the mother, and the resultant discontent in the slave quarters are three good reasons why not.

Slaves were, however, sometimes sold. Most sales were due to the death of a plantation owner. The slaves were property, and were sold in the course of the liquidation of the estate. Another instance was if there were more slaves than there was work, either through an increasing slave population, or due to a temporary bad market for the products of the plantation.

General remarks

The surprising fact about slavery and indentured servitude is not that they existed, but that they vanished in such a relatively short period of time. These forms of servitude were acceptable to most of the world for around four thousand years. Slavery was legally abolished in its last bulwark, the Arabian Peninsula, in 1962, yet it is still practiced illegally in some areas of the world. Slavery is recorded in the Book of Genesis: Some members of Abraham's household were slaves, and it was condoned by leading writers of the Western World as late as the latter half of the eighteenth century. Plato, in '**The Republic**,' envisioned the perfect society as a few free citizens and many slaves. Aristotle, the famous Greek educator and teacher of Alexander the Great, considered slavery part of the natural order of life. He said: 'From the hour of their birth some are marked out for subjection, others for rule.' The 'Golden Age of Greece' and 'The Grandeur That Once Was Rome' were built securely upon slave labor: An estimated 90% of the population were slaves.

The Roman Catholic Church has been a major owner and dealer in slaves. Pope

45

Gregory XI advocated slavery as a just punishment for any who resisted the Papacy. In 1375, he ordered that the excommunicated Florentines be sold into slavery whenever they were captured by Papal soldiers. About one hundred years later Pope Innocent VIII accepted a gift of one hundred Moorish Slaves from the king of Spain. Thomas More believed that slavery was the appropriate state for the underprivileged, common laborers, and criminals. He included the slavery class in his visionary book '**Utopia**.'

In 1525, when the Swabian serfs applied for emancipation from their slavery because 'Christ had died to set men free,' Martin Luther was as horrified as the Catholic Church. John Locke, who believed in the 'inalienable rights of man,' wrote a provision for slavery in his draft of the '**Fundamental Constitutions of Carolina**.' He also was an investor in the Royal African Company that held the British monopoly in the slave trade. John Locke believed that 'the origin of slavery, like the origin of liberty and property, was entirely outside the social contract' and 'If the hardships of bondage should at any time outweigh the value of life, a slave could commit suicide by resisting his master and receiving the death which he had all along deserved.' In 1700, a Puritan, Judge Sewell, opened the anti-slavery attack with his tract '**The Selling of Joseph**.' From then until 1774, strong ground work was laid by anti-slavery individuals. In that year, 1774, the English Society of Friends voted to expel any member involved in the slave trade. A little over a hundred years later, by 1888, slavery had vanished from its last holdout in the Americas - Brazil. Slavery, which lasted for more than four thousand years, supported by many famous individuals and strong institutions, had been outlawed by most modern nations in fewer than a hundred years.

THE PLANTATIONS

When Spain regained the Floridas in 1783 the vast majority of East Floridas citizenry, who were British subjects, left for Canada, England or the Bahamas. As the English, during their 20 year tenure in Florida, had begun a strong agricultural based society their departure left a void in the area. One of the ordinances of the Spanish government, in 1783, was that all the citizens of the Floridas had to be subjects of Spain. This meant that each individual had to be a Roman Catholic and a subject of the Spanish Crown. These stringent regulations made it difficult for Spain to find many persons who would be willing to settle in and colonize the province. This inability to attract settlers caused East Florida's economy to stagnate so in the early 1800s these laws were somewhat modified so that an individual did not have to be a subject of the Catholic church. The incorporation of these modifications regarding settlement policies, during the governorship of Enrique White, enticed a few immigrants into East Florida. These people settled south of St. Augustine in the Halifax-Hillsborough river area. One of the first of these colonists was Ambrose Hull from Connecticut. In 1801 he received two land grants totaling 2600 acres in the New Smyrna area. Before he was able to establish a working plantation he was driven out by Indian raids. He moved up to St. Augustine and began planning another settlement in the same place. During this time the Bahamas were experiencing an economic depression. Many of the British subjects who had left Florida in 1783 for the Bahamas now returned to East Florida under the liberalized immigration policy of the Spaniards. Individually, these families were afraid that the Indians would force them off their land grants; but they felt that if there were several well protected plantations in their vicinity, the Seminoles would not dare attack.

Within the Halifax-Hillsborough River area of East Florida, settlers began arriving to establish a plantation system. The backbone of this plantation system would soon be the money crops of sugar cane and indigo. Among the families who received land grants from the Spanish government were the Ambrose Hulls, 2600 acres; Samuel Williams, 3200 acres (after Samuel Williams died, his widow, Ana Marie Hill, married Joseph Hernandez. He later became a leading politician, planter and military leader in East Florida.); John Addison, 1800 acres (later exchanged for 1414 acres on the Tomoka River); Robert McHardy, 1000 acres on Turnbull River (Spruce Creek) and 1000 acres on the Tomoka River; James Ormond, 2000 acres; James Kerr, 1800 acres; Lindsay Todd, 600 acres; J. Munzo, 2400 acres; Charles Ceta, 2000 acres; John Bunch, 2110 acres; Patrick Dean, 1168 acres; and Samuel Betts, 2000 acres.

When land grants were sold or transferred, many legal or family disputes developed, and when the United States took over the Floridas in 1821 many claimants for land title could not be verified. The cause of family or legal disputes and lack of verification was vagueness in the wording of 'land grant.' This vagueness of title is shown in the request of Joseph Hernandez, 7 September 1824, to the United States requesting clear title to land along the

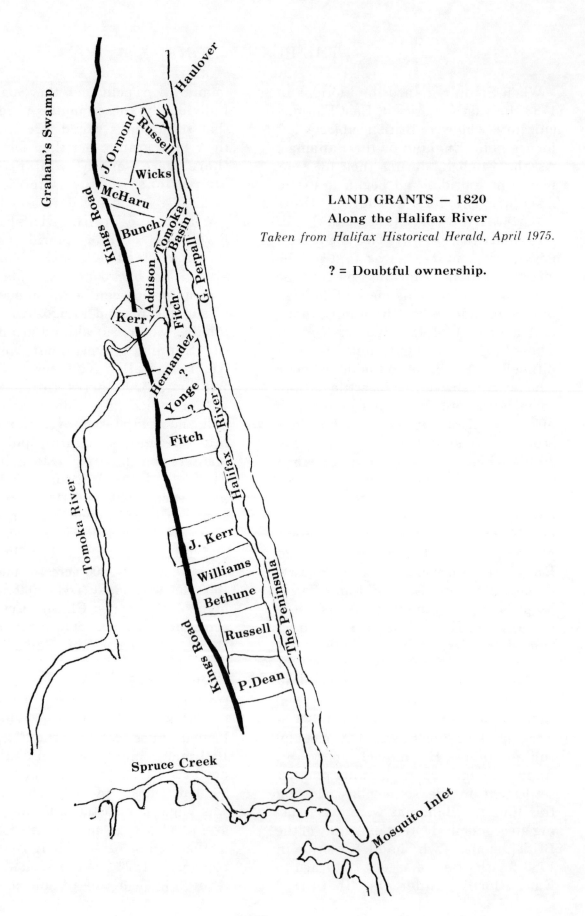

LAND GRANTS — 1820
Along the Halifax River
Taken from Halifax Historical Herald, April 1975.

? = Doubtful ownership.

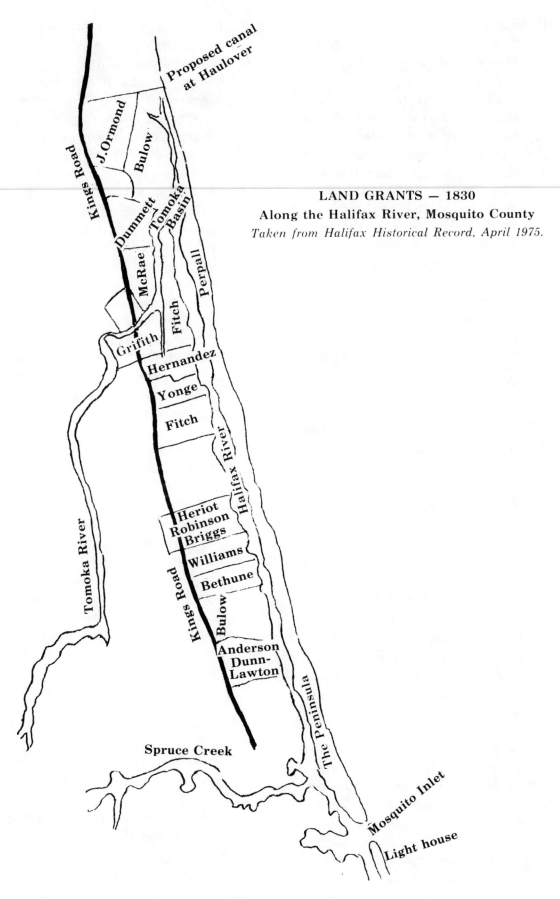

LAND GRANTS — 1830
Along the Halifax River, Mosquito County
Taken from Halifax Historical Record, April 1975.

Proposed canal
at Haulover

Kings Road

J. Ormond

Bulow

Dummett

Tomoka Basin

Perpall

McRae

Fitch

Grifith

Hernandez

Yonge

Fitch

Halifax River

Heriot
Robinson
Briggs

Williams

Bethune

Kings Road

Bulow

Anderson
Dunn-
Lawton

Tomoka River

The Peninsula

Spruce Creek

Mosquito Inlet

Light house

Halifax River.

The memorial of Joseph M. Hernandez respectfully showeth:

That your memorialist claims title to a tract of the river Halifax at a place called the Old Chimneys bounded on the west by the river Halifax. The first line begins at a pine, and runs south 68 degrees west, 20 chains, to a stake; the second line, thence runs north 22 degrees west, 100 chains to another pine; third line, thence north 68 degrees west 20 chains to another pine; fourth line, along the banks of the river, which title your memorialist derives from a concession made to Ana Marie Hill by Governor Estrada, August 19, 1811 in virtue of the royal order of 1790 as will appear by the public archives; that your memorialist having married the said Ana Marie Hill, cleared and cultivated it; and your memorialist further showeth that he is in actual possession of the said lands, and a citizen of the United States.

James M Hernandez

The legal description of Addison's 1414 acres along the Tomoka River was equally vague: 'bounded on the north by the public road, south by the lands of Gabriel Williams Perpall, and east by the river Tomoka.'

The plantations were expected to be almost completely self-sustaining. To be both self-sufficient and produce revenue the proprietors in the East Florida area expected to have oil, grapes, sugar, indigo, corn, rice, potatoes, all types of vegetables, and tropical fruit. They also expected to have poultry, cattle, hogs, horses and possibly mules. All the operating plantations had to have craftsmen to maintain the buildings and equipment. Each community needed a blacksmith for all the necessary metal work and a miller to grind the grain into flour. These two occupations, the blacksmith and miller, were indispensable to any community. For a plantation system, or a homesteader, to effectively be self-sustaining required a minimum of five acres per individual under cultivation. This allowed room for corn, vegetables, citrus, sugar cane and other produce plus space for animals.

The homesteader was at a disadvantage from the large property owner in that while the plantation proprietor was able to have, or train, various craftsmen to maintain the property, the homesteader had to know a little about many crafts. To be self-sustaining, the homesteader had to have tools, equipment and some knowledge of blacksmithing, construction, animal husbandry, milling, lumbering, agriculture plus many other crafts.

When Ponce de Leon heard rumors of a Fountain of Youth, he left all behind him and searched in vain through Florida for that fabulous water which had the power to rejuvenate a person. The early settlers did not come in search of that miraculous fountain, they came for land, space to grow, and for the possibility of wealth.

When they settled in East Florida they found plants with astounding powers. They observed the many uses the Indians made of the saw palmetto: The branches of any plant could be used for protection from the wind and sun; the dried wood could be used as fuel for fire, but they were surprised when they noticed that the Indians were eating or sucking on fresh picked berries from the palmetto plant. After watching and

Usual blacksmith forge and equipment found on all plantations and in all frontier communities in the early days of the United States.

51

questioning the Indians, the settlers found that the berries were an excellent balm for sore throats and congested noses. The berries would be picked when they were ripening, juice would then be extracted and when cured the syrup would be a very dark color and quite strong in flavor. This syrup could then be bottled and carried by the Indian or settler and used whenever needed. However, there were some hazards in picking this medicinal berry for the saw palmetto would lacerate the hands and legs of the picker, tear their clothing and even damage shoes. Frequently pickers were bitten by rattlesnakes lying in the shade near the base of the plants. An interesting extra benefit was accidentally discovered by some of the homesteaders: It seemed that the native birds enjoyed eating these berries; after consuming many of them, the birds could not always fly in a straight line. In fact quite often the birds could not fly at all, but walked dizzily in circles away from the berries. The settlers also noticed that the black bears enjoyed eating these ripened berries off the ground. The bears seemed to go wild, they would go on a rampage tearing up fields or ripping through buildings. Sometimes they would even break into occupied dwellings and chase the inhabitants out. Quite soon the homesteader found out that in addition to its medicinal values these berries, once fermented in the sun, became highly intoxicating to any who ate them. So now, from the very same plant, the settler was able to have an excellent cough and sore throat medicine plus an alcoholic beverage.

Another useful, undomesticated, plant they found was a bush that bore pods approximately 12 inches in length. When small and about 4 inches long the pods were edible. The foliage and the pods were also good as fodder for their animals. Once dried the pod was able to soak up moisture like a sponge, could be used to clean kitchen utensils, household furnishings and to scrub a person's skin. The sponge-scrubbers wore out quickly but were free for the picking in the settlers' backyard. This plant, the loufah, is still obtainable from seed stores.

From the pine tree the settler obtained turpentine and tar, from which cough syrup, dressing for wounds and bug or insect repellant was made. The potato, in addition to being an edible plant, was used as a cure for different ailments. A raw slice applied to a wart was thought to dry out the infection and allow the wart to drop off. To cure rheumatism, a potato would be carried in the pocket of the person who had this illness. To be more effective a poultice made out of a raw, peeled and grated potato helped cure rheumatism and drew poisons from wounds or abrasions. Herbal medicine was quite useful in any frontier community where there were few doctors and most of those available just believed in bleeding and amputation.

Each settler, whatever his status in life, first planted any vegetables he brought with him. These vegetables usually consisted of corn, sweet potatoes, beans, tomatoes, and any other easily grown plants. Once the land was cleared and food planted, a cabin was built from the fallen pine or oak. Often the settlers made hardwood wedges out of dried dogwood. These wedges were necessary to aid them in splitting lumber. To have wood good and straight enough for building living qurters the settler had to be able to know how to 'read' the tree. To do this the person had to carefully inspect the outside of the tree trunk. If there were any deep indentations or knobs the settler knew that the inside of the trunk would contain similar markings and be scarred. The most perfect trunks were used for the floors and walls of the living quarters, the less perfect were for bracing for the quarters. Other wood or lumber would be used for fencing and the least desirable or scraps would be used for fire wood.

Settlements, plantations and homesteads were established within easy walking distance of one or more of East Floridas' many free flowing rivers and streams. These waterways greatly aided in the transportation of supplies coming in and the shipping out of cash crops to worldwide markets. Two of the cash crops which made the plantation system profitable were indigo and sugar cane production. Sugar cane was also profitable for the small homesteader. It was possible to realize an average yield of 2000 pounds or two hogsheads (1000 pounds per hogshead) per acre. The

All plantations and most settlers' cabins had an area set aside for the spinning wheel and the sewing basket.

Stephanie Kaye Ervin

planter not only realized sugar from the cane but also rum and molasses. It cost around one to two cents per pound to produce and the grower was able to realize a large profit: Sugar was selling for around fourteen cents a pound in the early 1800s. Europe was embroiled in the Napoleonic Wars, in the Mediterranean area the Barbary pirates were causing havoc to shipping and in the economically depressed Caribbean area there were slave uprisings. This world economic situation allowed those areas able to produce sugar to get the price they asked.

Sugar cane fields were readied for planting in the early months of the year. Right after this, around March in East Florida, seed cane was planted or ratooned from the root of the previous year's crop. Seed cane came from the joints in the cane stalk. In October when the first cane of the cutting year was harvested it was placed in shallow furrows and covered with a light covering of earth. This covering would protect the cane from any winter freezing and also give it time to be ready for the spring planting. Harvesting the remainder of the crop continued through February. It was this first cane that was called seed cane. As the cane stalk lay in the shallow furrow shoots would grow from the joints. These shoots became the next year's seed and seed was planted around March. For cane to be ratooned, the stalk was cut near the earth and then the stump was lightly covered with dirt. From this stump another year's growth of sugar cane could be realized. In East Florida cane could be ratooned approximately five years without the sugar content being diminished. After the first cane was cut for seed or ratooning the farmer set the field on fire. This burning of the cane was done for at least three reasons: (1) To clean out any reptiles or animals that lurked in the cane field, (2) To give more working room for the field hands and, (3) To enhance the flavor of the forthcoming sugar.

Once cut, the cane was placed on carts and hauled to the sugarhouse. There it was fed through rollers and the extracted juice ran into barrels. On small farms the sugar mill was usually turned by mules, horses or oxen whereas on the larger plantations it was operated by steam engine. These steam engines could cost more than three thousand dollars. On elaborate sugar plantations, the juice, instead of running into barrels, went through copper tubes or wooden runways dropping into large vats or kettles. Always before entering the kettles the juice went through a filter system which collected large particles of impurities. (The kettles on Gambles plantation on the gulf coast could contain up to six hundred gallons of liquid.) This process of eliminating impurities was called clarification; the next stage was evaporation. In the evaporation stage, the juice flowed into large iron or copper kettles. There were four or five kettles on most sugar plantations. These were lined up in order of size. The first was the 'Grande,' the second 'Propre,' the third 'Flambeau,' the forth 'Syrup,' and the fifth 'Batterie.' On farms with only four kettles the Propre was eliminated. The furnace in the sugar house was positioned so that an even flow of heat reached each kettle. When raw cane juice entered the 'Grande' kettle, a small amount of slaked lime was added. This slaked lime acted as a catalyst which forced any remaining impurities to the surface where they could be skimmed off with large wooden spoons. When the foreman felt that all the impurities possible to get, had been skimmed off, he had the

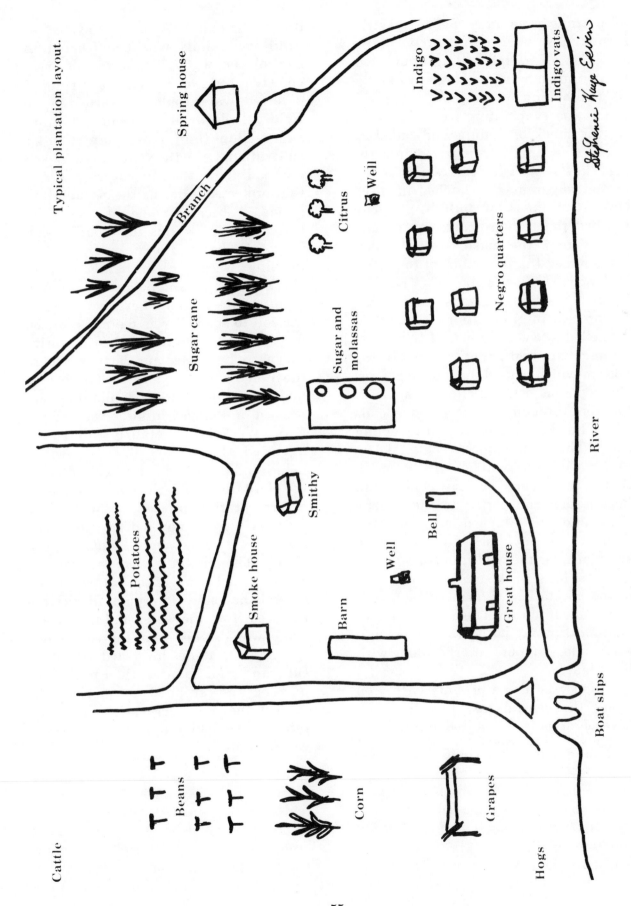

Typical plantation layout.

Spring house

Branch

Indigo

Indigo vats

Stephenie Hugo Ervin

Sugar cane

Citrus

Well

Negro quarters

Sugar and molassas

River

Potatoes

Smithy

Smoke house

Well

Bell

Barn

Great house

Boat slips

Cattle

Beans

Corn

Grapes

Hogs

55

juice transferred into the next kettle. Impurities were constantly being skimmed off as the boiling liquid was being transferred from kettle to kettle. As the boiling of the juice continued, water was evaporating from the mass. As the mass of boiling and bubbling liquid was finally transferred into the last kettle — the 'Batterie' — the master sugar maker watched intently. Once the mass of bubbling syrup reached the right consistency, around 232 degrees, the master sugar maker commanded that the moment to 'strike' had arrived. The 'strike' was reached when the solidifying mass had begun the process of granulation. It was then funnelled into cooling vats. The wooden cooling vats had slight crevices in the bottom which caused them to be porous. These porous bottoms allowed molasses to seep through and into hogsheads which had been placed under the cooling sugar. This curing process could take up to thirty days to complete. At the end of that time the cured sugar was placed in hogsheads, transported to the nearby river, and then shipped out to market. Some of the molasses was kept as a sweetener for the field hands and other workers. Most of the molasses was sent to the plantation or farm still where it was made into rum. The rum was either kept for drinking purposes or, if enough was made, sent out to market along with the sugar.

Indigo was also a primary cash crop along the central east Florida coast. Like sugar cane, it required quite a bit of moisture, yet too much dampness would drown the plants. A complex system of drainage canals was constructed to control the water. These canals were constructed so that if a drought occurred, water could be returned to the fields. Indigo fields required more supervision than most plants under cultivation. Once the young plant poked its head above the fine covering of dirt that protected it during the germination period, it became constant prey from caterpillars, cutworms and other insects. It was also liable to be choked by the fast growing weeds. Field hands had to check the plants and fields daily for any type of infestation. They also checked the soil to see if it was too moist or too dry. Once the plants reached maturity they were harvested and carted to where the indigo vats were located. The leaves, and sometimes the entire plants, were bruised and placed in large water-filled vats. Workers constantly stirred or agitated the water. This agitation helped indigo crystals to percolate out of the plant fiber. Once the plant completed a fermentation process, in which the crystals were removed from the plant fiber, the workers stopped agitating the water. The crystals were allowed to settle to the bottom of the vat. When the crystals had settled the plant fibers were removed from the water and the excess water was drained from the vats. Once the indigo granules hardened they were cut into small squares, then packed in barrels and shipped to market. At market the indigo crystals were made into beautiful blue dye for all types of woven material.

Settler taking baled goods to port.

PERFIDY
1783 - 1819

'This bill is brought by the Cherokee nation, praying an injunction to restrain the State of Georgia from the execution of certain laws of that state, which, as is alleged, go directly to annihilate the Cherokee as a political society, and to seize for the use of Georgia, the lands of the nation which have been assured to them by the United States, in solemn treaties repeatedly made and still in force. . . Though the Indians are acknowledged to have an unquestionable, and heretofore unquestioned, right to the lands they occupy. . .' However, 'they occupy a territory to which we assert a title independent of their will, which must take effect in point of possession.'

Chief Justice Marshall, 1831, Supreme Court Decision;
Cherokee Nation vs. Georgia.

All of our Indian troubles were caused originally by bad white men, if the truth were known. Indians rarely commit outrages unless they are first provoked to them by the border whites.

Kit Carson Cellis: **Life of Kit Carson.**

In 1783 the American Revolution was over. At the signing of the Treaty of Paris, Florida reverted to Spanish control. One stipulation of this treaty that would cause border disputes between the United States and Spain was that of the boundary of West Florida. The Treaty of Paris stated that the northern boundary of West Florida would be at the 31st parallel. During the British period, that boundary was located at the 32°28′ parallel. When Florida reverted to Spanish control, Spain wanted the boundary to remain as it was when the British controlled the territory. However the United States refused to accept any change in the treaty. An outgrowth of this refusal to change the northern boundary of West Florida was a Spanish blockade of traffic on the Mississippi River. She would not allow Americans free access to the river which led into the heartland of the United States. After more than ten years of bickering over free navigation of the Mississippi River and the northern boundary of Florida, Spanish Minister Godoy and American Secretary Thomas Pinckney negotiated a treaty between the two powers. The treaty, signed on October 27, 1795, concerned 'Friendship, Boundaries, Commerce and Navigation between the United States of America and the King of Spain.' Article 2 of the treaty stipulated that the northern boundary of West Florida would be the 31st degree north latitude. Article 4 opened the Mississippi River for free navigation to citizens of the United States. Even with the signing of

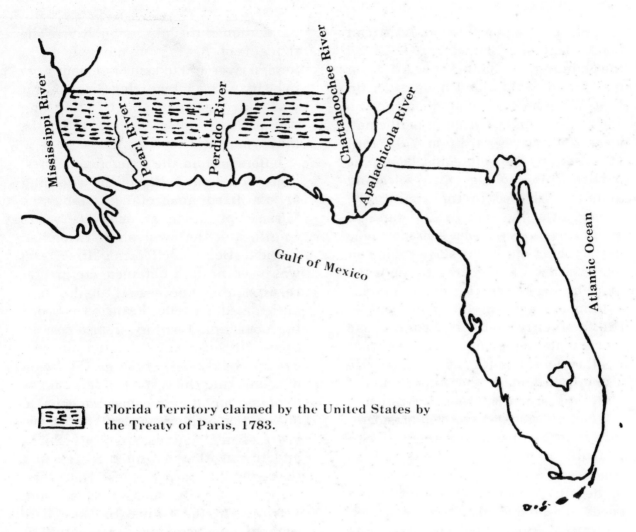

Mississippi River

Pearl River

Perdido River

Chattahoochee River

Apalachicola River

Atlantic Ocean

Gulf of Mexico

Florida Territory claimed by the United States by the Treaty of Paris, 1783.

this treaty of friendship, many people in the United States were not satisfied. They wanted all of Florida, and all other Spanish controlled provinces in the western hemisphere. They would sanction any organization that would dispute Spanish control of her provinces in this area.

It is fair to say that the generation that sows the seeds of war is seldom the one that reaps the harvest. The 2nd Seminole War and the Civil War (War for Southern Independence) were no exceptions to that rule. Many of the seeds for those two wars were sown during the days following the American Revolution. In the election of 1800 the Republican Party (present day Democratic Party) came into power. It

was voted into power by a sectional vote. The southern states voted almost as a block with 48 votes going to Jefferson and 4 going to Adams. The northern states also showed a unified trend with 39 votes going to Adams and 20 votes going to Jefferson. One reason Jefferson received this unified vote was his oft repeated expansionist ideas, and the southern states were expansion minded.

On March 4, 1801, Thomas Jefferson was sworn in as the president of the United States. The ceremony took place in the not yet finished new capital in Washington, D.C. The city was planned in 1792 during the first term of President George Washington. He had appointed a French immigrant, Pierre l'Enfant, to oversee the layout of the nation's capital. He also appointed an American black, Benjamin Banneker, to assist in the planning. Mr. Banneker was born on his parent's Maryland plantation in 1731. When he reached manhood he was one of the country's leading mathematicans and surveyors. From 1792 until 1802, four years before his death, he published one of this nation's leading almanacs related to forecasting the movement of the planets and stars. To aid in this project, he cut a circular hole in the roof of one of the slave cabins on his property. From gazing through the hole he was able to make precise notations regarding the movement of the heavenly bodies. From these movements he made fairly accurate weather forecasts for his almanac. He also included much other information of vital interest to the farmer and rancher.

When Jefferson was elected president, many of his backers wanted to see Florida and New Orleans under American control. They wanted outlets to the gulf coasts for their manufactured goods and produce. The territory which Georgia ceded to the federal government, after the revolution, was soon to become the states of Mississippi and Alabama. The federal government was aware that the area was rapidly attracting population. The rivers of these future states ran through the Spanish province of Florida and it was necessary, at any cost, for Florida to become part of the United States. The most expedient method of obtaining Florida would have been by means of a war of conquest, but that would have drawn the European powers of England and France into the fray on the side of Spain. There was no way a fledgling United States could have stopped the combined power of these nations.

In the Treaty of 1795, with Spain, the United States was provided free navigation of the Mississippi River. The thought of having to navigate on a foreign river and to load or unload cargo in a city with a foreign flag flying over it was outrageous to the free-thinking boatmen who plied their trade on the Mississippi River.

Jefferson, and the Republican Party, began a patient policy in the obtaining of his fixed goal of controlling the Mississippi River, through its entire length, and the ownership of Spanish Florida. Before Jefferson's first term was over he had obtained far greater results and success than he had anticipated. In 1800, France was ceded the Louisiana Territory from a coerced Spain. Napoleon knew that the only way France could realize her age old dream of conquering the British Isles would be to have a naval force somewhat equal to one of the English fleets. After a few years of negotiations, first with Spain and then with the United States, and then playing each against the other, Napoleon finally sold the Louisiana Territory to the United States. There were three conventions to the treaty: The first ceded Louisiana to the United States, the second was a payment of 60,000,000 francs to France, and the third was that the United States would assume any claims the citizens of the United States had against France. With the money Napoleon received from the sale of Louisiana, he had a naval fleet constructed. After a short time afloat this French naval force met the British fleet at Trafalgar. The rest was history: England controlled the seas and France the European continent until Waterloo.

In the ratification of this treaty with France were sown some of the seeds which would grow and result in the Civil War, others grew to help ignite the Seminole Wars. Jefferson, in a letter to Senator Breckinridge of Kentucky, said:

Objections are raising to the eastward (meaning the New England states) against the vast extent of our boundaries, and propositions are made to exchange Louisiana, or part of it, for the Floridas. But, as I have said, we shall get the Floridas without (trading for it), and I would not give one inch of the waters of the Mississippi to any nation.

The Congressional debate on the legality of the United States possession of a foreign territory was primarily a sectional one. Only four southern votes were recorded as opposed to carrying out resolutions necessary to implement the treaty ceding Louisiana to the United States. The four votes came from the State of Virginia. During the debates regarding the Louisiana Purchase, the northern states were strong champions of a strict interpretation of the Constitution, whereas the southern states were quite liberal in their views.

Possibly because of the acquisition of the Louisiana Territory and his having kept us out of any European entaglements, Jefferson was re-elected, with a sweeping vote of confidence. The electoral vote in the 1804 election was 162 for Jefferson and 14 for Pickney. During his first term in office, Jefferson had obtained one of his goals: Secure navigation of the Mississippi from its source to its mouth, and he had extended the western frontier to the Rocky Mountains. In his second term he hoped that he would be able to secure another goal: That of having gulf coasts ports readily available to the citizens of Georgia and the Mississippi Territory (present day Alabama and Mississippi). He had three courses open to him in realizing this goal: First — seizing Florida by open warfare with a weak Spain. This would bring France into the conflict on the side of Spain and could lead to a confrontation with England, 2nd — Try to obtain Florida by negotiation (this was the selected course), and 3rd —Tied in with the course of negotiation would be that of intensifying boundary disputes, and the insidious harassment of Florida's Spanish citizens, whether they were white, red or black. Governmental authorities in the United States, at both federal and state levels, realized the weak military condition of Spain and would do all they could to exploit this weakness.

One source of irritation to the Americans was the Florida Indians. That is shown by many of the writings of that day which speak of the Seminoles committing depredations, even when protecting Spanish Territory, and of the their accepting runaway slaves from the Southern border plantations into their villages. Another source of irritation was the feeling that when France ceded Louisiana to the United States, she included all the land west of the Pearl River in the treaty.

Shortly after receiving the Louisiana Territory from the French, the United States government became involved in both internal and external affairs which kept the federal government from pursuing an active role in obtaining Spanish Florida. One foreign involvement was that caused by the Mediterranean pirates. Since the latter part of the 1700s the Moorish kingdoms of Northern Africa, or the Barbary pirates, had been extorting tribute from European nations for the privilege of sailing the Mediterranean Sea. Ships flying the United States flag were also subject to this tribute money. In 1803 the federal government dispatched Commodore Preble with a fleet to protect

American commerce. Captain Bainbridge, with the frigate Philadelphia, was sent to blockade Tripoli. Approaching Tripoli, he sighted a pirate vessel and immediately gave chase. The pirate vessel entered safely into Tripoli harbor and the American frigate began to turn away from the shore. Captain Bainbridge had his vessel too close to shore and was unable to safely turn around. The Philadelphia ran aground under the guns of a shore battery. The entire crew of the Philadelphia was captured by the Tripoli pirates. This attack on and capture of an American ship of war greatly incensed the public. The federal government's plan for obtaining Spanish Florida was temporarily set aside and our main objective became that of disciplining the Barbary pirates. In the last year of Jefferson's first term and the first part of his second term, the military direction of this country was pointed toward the destruction of the city of Tripoli.

President Jefferson strengthened the American Mediterranean fleet and ordered Commodore Preble to blockade the entire coast of the Kingdom of Tripoli, not just the city. The President then ordered General William Eaton, the American consul at Tunis, to contact the ruler of Upper Egypt, Hamet, who was an adversary of Yusef, the ruler of the Kingdom of Tripoli. General Eaton did obtain an alliance with Hamet. This ruler of Upper Egypt furnished the Americans a unit of Arab cavalry and seventy Greek soldiers. General Eaton, with a mixed army of Arab calvary, Greek soldiers, Tripolian rebels and American sailors left Alexandria on the 5th of March 1805. After a grueling march of a thousand miles across the desert he arrived at the Tripolian port city of Derne on the 25th of April. Yusef, the King of Tripoli, was approaching from the other side with a strong army. As these two land forces engaged in battle a division of the American fleet arrived. Caught between the shelling from the American ships and the attack from the land force, Yusef was forced to sue for peace. He was unable to retreat to his capital city because he lacked food and water for his men. With the surrender of Yusef, a treaty of peace was concluded between the Barbary States and the United States. However, one odd item in this peace treaty was the stipulation that the United States pay Yusef a sum of sixty thousand dollars for the liberation of the American slaves.

Internally, from 1804 to 1807, the United States was disturbed by the scheme of ex-Vice President Aaron Burr to raise an army for the invasion of Mexico. His plans called for conquering Mexico, then the taking of the western and southern states out of the union and the establishment of a southwestern empire. In February, 1807, Burr was arrested in Alabama and taken to Richmond to stand trial for treason. Burr was found 'not guilty, for want of sufficient proof.' Yet, his escape from death was so close, that he left the country under an assumed name. He returned a few years later and established a law practice in New York.

Jefferson's second term was fraught with external difficulties. England and France were embroiled in continuous war. This war between the two strongest powers in the world, at that time, gave the United States the opportunity to build a strong merchant fleet. While our merchant fleet was being expanded at a tremendous rate, our naval force was being neglected. Even though we basked in our victory over the small sailing vessels of the Barbary states, our navy was not equal to the task of meeting the

English fleet. The war with France had crippled and almost eliminated the English merchant fleet, since all their experienced sailing personnel were required on the English fighting ships. This allowed the United States merchant fleet to carry the bulk of the world's trade goods. As our merchant fleet was primarily located in the northeastern states, this brought a good deal of wealth to that section of the country. With Europe involved in a war to the death, it was the United States merchant ships which supplied both sides with military and civilian goods. Both England and France realized that it was the United States merchant fleet that kept their adversary supplied with the merchandise of war. However, it was France that benefited the most from the American trade since she had few merchant ships and less control of the seas.

In 1806, England declared the entire coast of France to be in a state of blockade. Any American vessels approaching France was seized by the British navy and condemned as a prize of war. These ships were to be sold to the highest bidder and the prize money to be divided between the English government and the crew of the capturing vessel. France quickly retaliated and declared a blockade of English ports. Now American vessels were at the mercy of the French vessels of war. During this time, independent ship owners could be issued Letters of Marque, which allowed their vessels to operate as privateers or as National Ships of War. The English blockade was soon increased to cover all of Europe. The United States Merchant Fleet quickly shrank into insignificance.

Once the American Merchant Fleet was forced to retreat into its own coastal waters, England became quite overbearing and arrogant. She declared that any person born an Englishman — was always an Englishman. Under this rule British Ships of War were authorized to stop and search any vessel found on the high seas and examine all persons on that ship. The British captain would then decide who aboard was an Englishman. The indignation of the citizens of the northeastern states was running quite high when an act of violence took place which made all Americans desire war with England.

A United States frigate, the **Chesapeake**, had just been outfitted in the Chesapeake Bay. The ship received orders to sail before all her guns were mounted. As soon as her captain took her out into the Atlantic Ocean, she was hailed by the British man of war **Leopard**. The **Chesapeake** hove to and British officers came on board. The British ordered Commodore Barron to muster the American crew so they could investigate for possible English deserters. Commodore Barron refused this, ordered the English off his vessel, and then cleared the **Chesapeake** for battle. Before the few guns that were mounted could be loaded and run out, the **Leopard** fired a destructive broadside. The Americans were compelled to surrender. The British officers came back on board the **Chesapeake** and took off four sailors. One was found to be a deserter from an English ship; he was hung. The other three, Americans, were freed after a length of time.

On December 21, 1807, President Jefferson passed the Embargo Act which detained all American ships in port. His idea was to cut off commercial enterprises between the United States and Europe. The Embargo Act helped cause more sectional bitterness, because the northeastern states suffered financial distress while the southern and western states were hardly affected. By early 1809, due to the Embargo Act, the British blockade of Europe and the French blockade of England, our merchant fleet was almost nonexistent.

These three events, the Barbary Pirates, the Burr Affair, and the action of England and France, kept the minds of President Jefferson, his administration and the governments of the southern states off of Spanish Florida until late 1809. The problem of obtaining Spanish Florida passed on to the successor of Thomas Jefferson, James Madison. Even though war continued in Europe, the eyes of many expansionists turned back to Florida.

Captain John Sprague said:

> It must be remembered that Florida, at the period reffered to, was an Indian border, the resort of a large number of persons, more properly temporary inhabitants of the Territory than citizens, who sought the outskirts of civilization to perpetuate deeds which would have been promptly and severely punished if committed within the limits of a well regulated community. They provoked the Indians to aggressions, and upon the breaking out of the war ignominiously fled or sought employment in the service of the General Government, and clandestinely contributed to its continuance.

Much of the agitation occurring along the border of Spanish Florida was caused by ruffians who temporarily lived along the southern border of Georgia and the Mississippi Territory. These cattle thieves and slave hunters kept the border in an uproar. Spain, beset with difficulties with France, was unable to send any military force to the new world to protect her possessions from armed aggression. She was only able to protect her American provinces by the word of their governors. As their verbal protestations could not be backed by any military strength, the border Americans, with the tacit approval of their state or territorial governments and approved by the federal administration, could continue their depredations with immunity.

In Europe, France turning against her old ally, Spain, invaded her and Napoleon placed his brother Joseph on the Spanish throne. During this period of confusion, the Spanish American colonies seized the opportunity to declare their independence. Britain, now on the side of Spain in the European war, caused much apprehension in the minds of American expansionists, for they were fearful that Spain might make a secret agreement with England and cede Spanish Florida to her. To preclude this possibility, American freebooters and immigrants in West Florida rebelled against the Spanish authorities. They seized the Spanish territory from the Mississippi River eastward to the Perdido River and declared West Florida a free and independent state. President James Madison refused to recognize the actions of these rebels, but he did signify that a Spain wracked by war was unable to hold on to her far flung provinces. So on October 27, 1810, President Madison proclaimed that the United States was taking possession of West Florida. He said the federal government ordered the occupation to save West Florida from anarchy and mischief and the anarchy and mischief he was saving West Florida from was caused by Americans. On December 7, Governor Claiborne

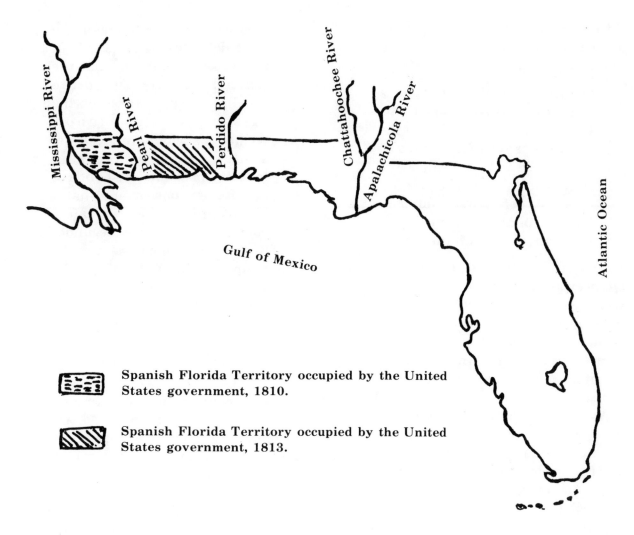

Mississippi River

Pearl River

Perdido River

Chattahoochee River

Apalachicola River

Atlantic Ocean

Gulf of Mexico

▨ Spanish Florida Territory occupied by the United
States government, 1810.

▨ Spanish Florida Territory occupied by the United
States government, 1813.

formally took possession of West Florida, but only occupied the land as far east as the Pearl River. In a message to Congress on December 5, President Monroe refers to the occupation of West Florida by saying:

> The Spanish authority was subverted, and a situation produced exposing the country to ulterior events which might essentially affect the rights and welfare of the Union. In such a conjuncture, I did not delay the interposition for the occupancy of the territory west of the River Perdido, to which the title of the United States extends, and to which the laws provided for the Territory of

Orleans are applicable.

Almost ten years before, President Jefferson had said that the United States would obtain Spanish Florida and slowly this was happening.

This usurpation of Spanish territory by the federal government caused quite a heated debate in Washington. During the debates a petition was submitted by the representative of the Territory of Orleans, which included occupied ex-Spanish West Florida, asking that the territory be admitted as a state. A bill for the purpose of admitting the Territory of Orleans as a state was submitted on December 27, 1810. The debate on this bill generated much sectional strife and more seeds were sown to be harvested in the Civil War. During the debate to admit Orleans, John Quincy of Massachusetts said:

> If this bill passes, it is my deliberate opinion that it is virtually a dissolution of this Union: that it will free the States from their moral obligation, and, as it will be the right of all, so it will be the duty of some, definitely to prepare for a separation, amicably if they can, violently if they must.

As we know, this statement of John Quincey's was vindicated, for the union was dissolved about fifty years later. Still by a sectional vote, the occupied Spanish Territory was admitted by the Territory of Orleans. In April 1812, the Territory of Orleans became the state of Louisiana.

As the citizens of the United States who were living, or more properly, encamped, along the border of Spanish West Florida used every means they could to appropriate that part of the Spanish province to their own use; so the Georgians who lived along the well-defined boundary separating Georgia from East Florida continued to cast covetous eyes upon the Spanish province of East Florida. To assist them in obtaining their desired goal of throwing the Spanish out, various individuals began banding together for the purpose of making incursions into Spanish territory. These individuals rustled Indian cattle, stole Indian slaves, kidnapped free blacks for sale on the auction block, and in general made life miserable for any inhabitant of Spanish East Florida. To give their approval of these individuals, the federal government in secret session on January 15, 1811, passed the following resolution:

Resolved by the Senate and House of Representatives of the United States of America, in Congress assembled, That the United States, under the peculiar circumstances of the existing crisis, cannot, without serious inquietude, see any part of the said territory pass into the hands of any foreign power; and that a due regard to their own safety compels them to provide, under certain contingencies, for the temporary occupation of the said territory; they, at the same time, declare that the said territory shall, in their hands, remain subject to future negotiations. Approved, January 15, 1811.

The 'peculiar circumstances' and 'existing crisis' mentioned in the resolution refer to the European conflict between England and France. As England and Spain were allied against Napoleonic France, the United States was quite fearful that a weak Spain would cede Florida to a strong England. This would put British power on both the northern and southern borders of the United States. It would also give England warm water ports much closer to the United States commerce than she now had. There was no way the federal, state or territorial governments in the United States could bear the thought of a vibrant power in Florida.

England, by this time, had outlawed the transportation of slaves, was quite strong on the seas and would hinder any pirate trade that flowed into the United States through the Fernandina area. Fernandina, the leading, really the only town on Amelia Island had been declared an open or duty free port by the Spanish authorities. This meant that no taxes or import duty was levied on any of the merchandise passing through their port. Fernandina had become an open city about five years earlier, right after President Jefferson, in 1807, had signed the Embargo Act. As this act closed all United States ports to shipping, vessels made for the nearest neutral port and then smuggled the merchandise into the United States. Fernandina was across the river from St. Marys, Georgia, and their location made it the perfect location for illegal operations. The lack of any governmental restrictions made it a wealthy town with approximately $500,000 profit each year going into the smuggler's pockets.

Marjory Douglas, writing of Amelia Island during this period, said:

> . . . Fernandina on Amelia Island was an even more riotous and busy center of smuggling. Slave dealers, pirates, adventurers and renegades swarmed there, crowding taverns, rum shops, gambling dens and brothels as sloops and schooners from Nassau and the West Indies jammed her sheltered waters.

Therefore, this secret resolution, which was a forerunner of the Monroe Doctrine, gave Georgians, any freebooter or thief tacit approval to overthrow the already weak Spanish government in Florida.

Lest it be thought that the southern and western parts of the United States had only expansionist views toward the Floridas, De Bow's Review for August 1850 reported: 'We have a destiny to perform, a manifest destiny over all Mexico, over South America, over the West Indies and Canada.' Though this opinion was written about forty years after President Madison signed the congressional resolution to occupy the Floridas, it still shows the thoughts and feelings of the expansionist of the early 1800s. In 1811 and 1812 a mania for invading and conquering Spanish Texas and Mexico swept the southern and western areas of the United States. Armies of liberation were springing up throughout the Mississippi Valley area. These armies flowed like a river through New Orleans and other parts of the Louisiana Territory toward Texas and Mexico. They all met a similar fate— defeat by the sun and sand or by the military might of Spain and Mexico. This mania for new lands to conquer was not appeased with the acquisition of Spanish Florida, but continued until the Civil War. Armies of hundreds and thousands still flowed out of the south and west to try to subdue Cuba, Mexico and Central America. When the Civil War was over, an ex-Confederate Army invaded Mexico to try to assist Maxmillian and so keep him in power. Many ex-Confederate families moved to Brazil and there carved out an area for their society which remains to this day. The majority of these expansionist adventures were aimed at enlarging or continuing the plantation system of the old south and west.

The congressional resolution to occupy the Spanish province of Florida was passed only after a heated debate. This debate, following the sectional lines which gave James Madison the 1808 election, helped sow more seeds of disunity which were reaped in 1861. In 1808 the New England states voted almost en bloc for the Federalist, or strict Constitutional group, whereas the southern and western states were virtually united in their support for the Republican (present day Democratic) or Liberal group. Even though England was stopping and searching American vessels of commerce on the high seas, and at times forcefully taking off American citizens to serve in her fleet, New England was strongly pro-English. This area, which was most adversely affected by England's high-handedness, did not take up one of the mottos of the southern and western expansionist: 'Free Trade and Sailors' Rights.' So when the secret resolution to obtain Spanish Florida (which was indirectly aimed at England) was introduced in Congress, the New England states were opposed.

With the passage and presidential signing of this joint resolution to control Florida, the way was clear for President Madison to complete one of the Jefferson administration's objectives — the control of Florida. Madison quickly appointed General George Matthews and Colonel John McKee as commissioners to enter into negotiations with the Spanish provincial governors, Governor Folch of West Florida and Governor Estrada of East Florida, for the peaceful surrender of their province.

One provision of their instructions stated:

> Should there be room to entertain a suspicion of an existing design in any foreign power to occupy the country in question, you are to keep yourselves on the alert, and, on the first undoubted manifestation of the approach of a force for that purpose, you will exercise with promptness and vigor the powers with which you are invested by the President, to preoccupy by force the territory, to the entire exclusion of the armament that may be advancing to take possession of it.

The commissioners were also informed that the Treasury Department would meet any financial drafts they issued and military and naval officers were instructed to obey their commands. To give such directions to the ex-governor of Georgia, and a general in the Georgia Militia, was quite dangerous. Georgians were in the forefront of almost all border attacks on East Florida, and were just waiting for any indication from the federal government that it would authorize any attempt to subvert the lawful authorities of East Florida. To facilitate the government's endeavor to take control of Spanish East Florida, General Matthews assembled an army in excess of 300 men. These well armed and undisciplined men were to ask the Spanish government to peacefully surrender their province to the United States.

What happened next with this army becomes a bit hazy and their actions depend on what is reported by the writers and what they wish to describe. The men under General Matthews are known as 'The Florida Revolutionists' or so-called Patriots. It is by the name Patriot that they have entered some of the Florida history books and also some of the diaries written at that time by the citizens of Spanish East Florida. This army assembled at the Georgia border town of St. Mary. Nearby, in Spanish Florida, was the port town of Fernandina, a city utilized by smugglers and slavers based on Amelia Island. General Matthews had received the impression from President Madison and members of Congress that if he captured Amelia Island the United States would be glad to annex it as part of Georgia.

When General Matthews asked the governor of East Florida to surrender his Spanish province to the United States, Governor Estrada refused.

Matthews then looked around to see if there was any indication that England was about to take control of the Floridas. He found no evidence of such intended action; and when the Spanish governor refused to surrender the province, General Matthews was temporarily thwarted. He quickly found an ally in Colonel John McIntosh, a St. Johns River plantation owner. A small group of Americans, aided by General Matthews' Georgians, organized a government which they called 'The Republic of East Florida.' Colonel McIntosh became General McIntosh and was elected governor of the republic. A Colonel Ashley was appointed commander of the rebels, calling themselves Patriots. He immediately moved on Fernandina and demanded the surrender of that city and Amelia Island, from the Spanish commander, Major Don Jose Lopez. Major Lopez had a military force of only 10 men to protect Amelia Island and the surrounding area. As the American bandits attacked the Spanish fortifications, nine American gunboats arrived and aimed their guns on the Spanish flag. These gunboats would not have been at that location without the express approval of the United States government. Major Lopez had the good sense to surrender to the American forces. The capitulation was made on March 17, 1812, and two days later on March 19th the island was turned over to Lieutenant Ridgely of the United States army.

The so-called 'Republic of East Florida' and the army of Patriots were nothing more than a cover for the naked aggression of the United States. Once Amelia Island was secured this army of Patriots, or more properly mercenaries, for each man had been promised 200 acres of Florida land once Spain was out, marched on to St. Augustine. On the way they were reinforced by around 100 men from the countryside. The governor of East Florida, Colonel Estrada, had received warning of this impending attack from George J.F. Clarke who had escaped the Patriots at Amelia Island. General McIntosh, with his Patriots, came down the Old Kings Road toward St. Augustine and encamped at the ruins of old Fort Mosa, just north of the capital of East Florida. Colonel Estrada with his men, and volunteers from the plantations around St. Augustine, met the American force and defeated them. The Americans retreated to the St. Johns River area and for more than a year plundered the countryside as far south as Mosquito Lagoon.

In a diary written between 1811 and 1823 we find a few entries regarding the Patriots. In the year 1812 we find these entries:

> The schooner **Ploughboy** arrived at Mosquito about the beginning of March, detained by contrary winds until the beginning of April, first intelligence at Mosquito of the patriots in East Florida — received the 17th March. Mr. McHardy and Mr. Addison come to Orange Grove the 23rd May. — Mr. McHardy had just returned from St. Augne. with letters. 24 May Mr. McHardy and Mr. Addison returned the same day were prevented from proceeding on their journey by a heavy hail storm about twelve miles from Orange Grove.

In July we find this entry:

> Mr. Williams and family came down to Orange Grove the 13th instant. Mr. McHardy left Orange Grove the next day. Mr

McHardy was arrested by the patriots and compelled to go with them to the camp 17th July. Mr. McHardy returned from camp 12 August.

These were the only references found in the diary which gave any indication that the Patriots were in the Mosquito Lagoon area and ravaging the province that far south. The writer of the diary seems to have lived on the Williams Plantation which was named 'The Orange Grove.' Present day Daytona Beach is located where the Williams Plantation was. Many of the well known people of that period are mentioned as guests at the Orange Grove, among them a Mr. Kerr and a Mr. Hernandez.

According to the diary, outrages on the citizens of Mosquito Lagoon were being caused by the Patriots thru August 1812. Four months before, in late March or early April, the federal government had received very strong protests from both the Spanish and British authorities condemning the United States for its actions in East Florida. This caused President Madison to repudiate the actions of General Matthews and say that he did not authorize an invasion of Spanish East Florida. On April 4, 1812 James Monroe, Secretary of State, wrote General Matthews saying:

> . . . But in consideration of the part which you have taken which differs so essentially from that contemplated and authorized by government, and contradicts so entirely the principle on which it has uniformly and sincerely acted, you will be sensible of the necessity of discontinuing the service in which you have been employed. You will, therefore,

consider your powers revoked on the receipt of this letter.

Governor Mitchell of Georgia replaced General Matthews as commissioner and was instructed to return all land conquered by the Americans to its rightful owner. This order to return Amelia Island and the other land was written April 10th, but, on May 27th Secretary Monroe instructed Governor Mitchell to hold Amelia Island during negotiations with the Spanish authorities. The reason given for this change in orders was fear of a British invasion. By this time, a force of Spanish Negroes had moved up from St. Augustine to re-occupy Amelia Island. They found Americans still in control of the area and began a short spirited skirmish. The American commander, Lieutenant Williams, and seven of his men were killed. The Spanish force withdrew after the engagement. Shortly after, the new Spanish governor, Kindelin, arrived and formally demanded that American forces be taken out of Spanish East Florida. In compliance with this request all American forces in East Florida, except those on Amelia Island, withdrew to American territory. Even though the regular United States military forces honored this request and left Florida, the Patriots remained and kept up their insidious pressure on the Spanish government.

Not only was pressure exerted on Spanish Florida along the East Coast, but also along the entire border where the Floridas met United States territory. During 1812 well planned raids by Georgians into Florida to capture Negroes and to weaken Spain's Indian allies were conducted with great frequency. Along the east coast, the Patriots captured Amelia Island from a defending Spanish force of ten men and then committed general havoc as far south as New Smyrna. Into Central Florida came another force of Georgians under the command of a Colonel Newman or Nunen who moved into what is now Alachua County. It had been reported among the Georgians that the central Florida Seminoles were planning a raid into Georgia. The villages of the Alachua Seminoles were some 75 miles inside Spanish Florida, in rich cattle raising country. The Georgia Militia, under Colonel Daniel Newman, numbered in excess of 300 men while the Seminole's warriors in the Alachua area were estimated at 150 men. The principal chiefs in this area were King Payne and Bowlegs. Both were sons of the Creek Indian Chief Secoffee who, around 1750, led a band of dissident Creeks into the central part of northern Florida after the Apalachees and Timucuan tribes were destroyed. When the Georgia Militia arrived at a lake a few miles from King Paynes Town, the Indians began a defensive attack from a hammock. It seems strange that if the Seminoles were planning a raid into Georgia they would allow an invading force to arrive so close to their principal

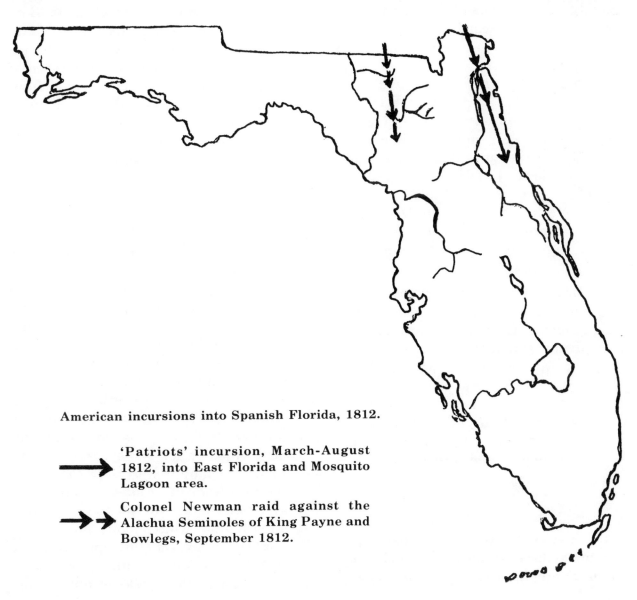

American incursions into Spanish Florida, 1812.

'Patriots' incursion, March-August 1812, into East Florida and Mosquito Lagoon area.

Colonel Newman raid against the Alachua Seminoles of King Payne and Bowlegs, September 1812.

town without trying to stop it earlier. For about ten days (eight days in one account and two weeks in another one) the Georgians and the Seminoles had a continuing running engagement. It was estimated that the Seminoles lost between 75 to 100 warriors with King Payne being wounded. (One account reported both King Payne and Billy Bowlegs as having been killed.) Colonel Newman retreated back into Georgia with only a portion of his command still intact. Every time United States forces invaded Spanish territory the Seminoles lost irreplaceable warriors. Slowly but surely the defenders of Spanish Florida were being weakened by these border incursions from their strong northern neighbor.

From 1783, when Spain regained Florida from Britain until the United States took control of the Floridas in 1821 there were many incidents of southern whites provoking the Indians and Spaniards. In addition, the Indians and Spaniards provoked the Americans into retaliatory raids. In December, 1812, Governor Kindelan of east Florida, in a letter to Governor Mitchell of Georgia, wrote:

> But the Indians you say — well, sir, why wantonly provoke the Indians, if you dislike their rifle and toma-hawk? General Matthews told Payne, in the square of Latchuo, that he intended to drive him from his lands, . . . The Indians are to be insulted, threatened, and driven from their homes; if they resist nothing less than extermination is to be their fate.

About twenty-five years before it occured, the governor of Spanish East Florida prophesied the general policy of the United States toward the Seminoles and toward most other Indian tribes.

Spanish difficulties with American intervention in their Florida territory did not end in 1812 when the federal government ordered the withdrawal of American forces from the area. In early 1813, American citizens forced a weak Spain to cede her lands west of the Perdido River to the United States. Even though Spain was an ally of England at this time, she was unable to stop the aggressive actions of her northern neighbor. About this time the United States constructed a small stockade about forty miles north of Mobile Bay, on the Alabama River, in the Mississippi Territory. This small military post was built for the purpose of keeping the peaceful Creeks from harming the settlers and to intimidate a weak Spain. In 1813 this fort, Fort Mims, was commanded by Major Daniel Beasley. Major Beasley would rather have been up north fighting the English than stationed at this out-of-the-way post. He wanted action and he would soon get more than he bargained for. Tecumseh, the Shawnee chief from the Ohio Valley, had recently made a trip through the Creek Territory trying to unify the Indians for a general uprising against the Americans. Tecumseh had been somewhat coddled by the British, who had made him a brigadier general in their army. The Indians of the north and those from the southeast were of different racial stock and they seldom got together for anything except to fight each other or for trade purposes. The Alabama Indians were very cool to the overture from the Shawnees and there was really no reason for the more than three million whites along the western frontier to expect the approximately 18,000 Indians to rise up against them. Even though the Creeks would not join

72

the Shawnees, they had been pushed around quite a bit by the settlers who wanted Indian land. One group of Creeks was known as Red Sticks: Each of the warriors carried a red stick, possibly for religious reasons. Major Beasley had been warned many times that the Red Sticks were upset and were planning to attack the fort. He took no notice of the impending attack, but on August 30, 1813, he wished he had. On that day the Creeks under Wetherford attacked the fort and the civilian cabins around it. Of the approximately 550 Americans in the area, more than 400 were slain. One of the best descriptions regarding this attack is found in the novel **Oh, Promised Land** by James Street. The news of this attack, or massacre, quickly spread throughout the southeast. The governors of Tennessee, Georgia and the Mississippi Territory immediatley called out their militias and made plans to invade Creek Territory.

General Andrew Jackson had recently been badly wounded in a gun duel with the Benton brothers. He was recovering from these wounds when he was asked to take command of the forces being mustered to fight the Creek Red Sticks who numbered less than four thousand. Fewer than one third of the Indians were armed with muskets, and they had very little powder and lead. By October 11th Jackson began moving against this less than formidable foe. A force of nine hundred men under Colonel (some accounts read General) Coffee attacked the Indian village of Tallushatchee and killed every Indian they found. The following month, November 8th, the Americans met a force of Creeks at Talladega. Again the Indians were soundly defeated and forced to retreat. Davy Crockett, one of the Tennessee volunteers, reported that the Indians were 'shot like dogs.'

During December 1813, and January 1814, the militia became rebellious and wanted to return home. Their terms of enlistment, mostly for 90 days, had expired. In addition, they had been on short rations for some time: By early January they were eating acorns. In mid January Jackson had his troops formed up and gave them a stirring speech, telling them they were there to keep the redskins from scalping, killing and maiming white settlers. After the speech Jackson drew his pistols and said that he would personally shoot any volunteer who tried to go home. None, of course, left that day.

On January 22nd they fought the Creeks at Emucface and pushed them toward a place called Tohepeka. The whites called the location Horseshoe Bend because the Tallapoosa River winds northward and westward enclosing a large tract of land in the form of a peninsula having a narrow neck. The Indians fortified the area with great skill and resourcefulness — they knew this would be their last stand. During early March Colonel Coffee, with his command, fortified the east and south banks of the Tallapoosa to prevent the Creeks from crossing over to escape. General Jackson, with the main force, was on the north and west side of the river thus effectively enclosing the Creek warriors, their wives and children. By March 26th all was in readiness and on the 27th the Americans began the Battle of Horseshoe Bend. According to Ridpath's **History of the United States**, published in 1884:

> On the 27th of March, the main body of whites under General Jackson stormed the breast-works and drove the Indians into the bend. There, huddled

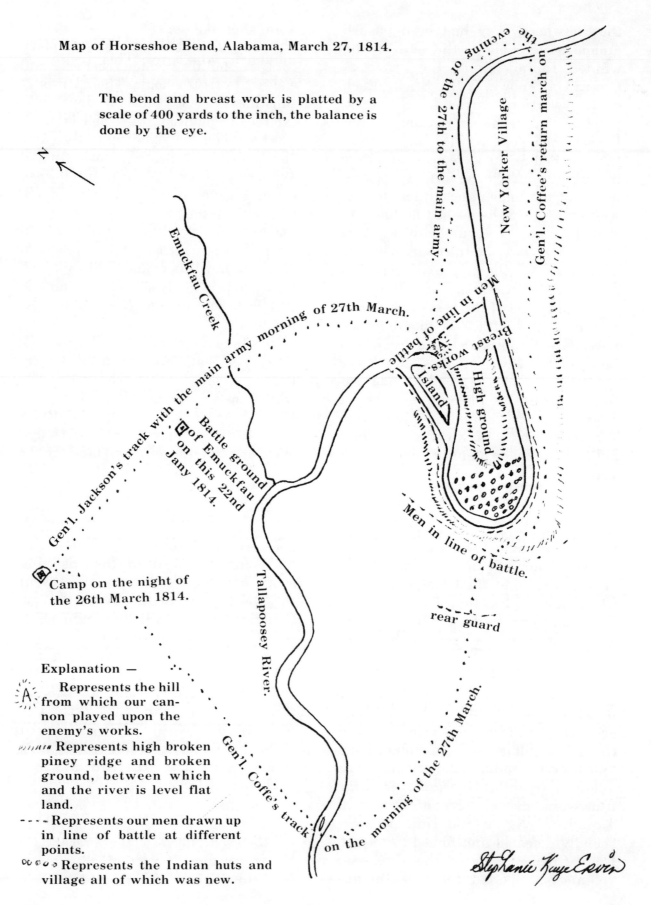

Map of Horseshoe Bend, Alabama, March 27, 1814.

The bend and breast work is platted by a scale of 400 yards to the inch, the balance is done by the eye.

N

Emuckfau Creek

Gen'l. Jackson's track with the main army morning of 27th March.

Battle ground of Emuckfau on this 22nd Jany 1814.

Camp on the night of the 26th March 1814.

Tallapoosey River.

Gen'l. Coffe's track

on the morning of the 27th March.

Men in line of battle.

Island

Breast works

High ground

New Yorker Village

Men in line of battle.

Gen'l. Coffee's return march on the evening of the 27th to the main army.

rear guard

Explanation —

A Represents the hill from which our cannon played upon the enemy's works.

Represents high broken piney ridge and broken ground, between which and the river is level flat land.

- - - - Represents our men drawn up in line of battle at different points.

Represents the Indian huts and village all of which was new.

Stephanie Kaye Ervin

74

together without the possibility of escape, a thousand Creek warriors, with the women and children of the tribe, met their doom.

The strength of the Creek Nation was destroyed and other Creeks in the Mississippi Territory sued for peace on any terms. Of course, the killing of Indian men, women and children is not referred to as a massacre in our history books as was the Massacre (?) of Fort Mims, where white men, women and children were killed by attacking Indian forces.

These victories against a weak foe made Jackson a hero in Washington and he was offered a regular army commission of brigadier general. Jackson was promised a brevet to the next major general vacancy. He accepted the commission as brigadier general and as luck would have it Major General William H. Harrison resigned his commission before Jackson had left Washington. Thus Jackson became a major general in command of the Seventh Military District. This district included everything west of the Alleghenies to the Mississippi River and from the Ohio River to the Gulf.

A point of interest: In the war against the Red Sticks, our allies were other Creek warriors. It is strange that in every Indian war this nation has fought, our major allies have always been Indians of the same or closely related tribes as those we fought. Once the peace treaty was signed, our Indian allies suffered the same fate as the losers.

After obtaining his commission as major general commanding the Seventh Military District, Jackson returned to the Mississippi Territory to prepare a peace treaty with the beaten Creeks. There was no discussion, no give and take, Jackson dictated the terms and the Indians had to agree. This Treaty of Fort Jackson (August,1814), was one of the harshest treaties in the history of this country. The terms were so onerous that the Indians violated the treaty as soon as they could. Jackson knew how cruel the treaty was, for he kept a force of United States regulars in the field to overawe the Creeks. As soon as they could, many Red Sticks fled south into Spanish Territory. These Creeks were the last major influx of Indians prior to the Seminole Wars. One of the Creeks who fled into Florida was a young boy named Powell or Osceola.

As mentioned earlier, Spain and England were allied against Napoleonic France. England, using the prerogative of an ally, used the port of Pensacola to rest and outfit her West Indies fleet. Spain was allied with England against France, but not against the United States. The Spanish governor, Don Matteo Gonzales Manrigue, protested to the English about their using Pensacola as a base against the Americans at Mobile and New Orleans. Spain was quite weak, and could do no more than offer verbal protests. When the Americans invaded East Florida in 1812 all Colonel Estrada could do was to ask the Americans to leave.

England, using her vastly superior might, seized Forts Barrancas and St. Michael, which guarded Pensacola harbor, and the governor's house in Pensacola. They acted more as conquerers than allies. In May, 1814, Captain George Woodbine, British Marines, was sent to the Apalachicola River area to train the local Indians for proposed warfare against the Americans. In August, the same month as the Treaty of Fort Jackson, Lt. Colonel Edward Nicolls, British

Marines, arrived in the same area with about a hundred men and took command of the operation. One of his projects was the construction of a fort at Prospect Bluff on the Apalachicola River. This fort was about sixteen miles up-river from the gulf and about sixty miles south of American territory. The fort was equipped with cannon, small arms and a large amount of ammunition. When Colonel Nicolls left Florida a few months later, the fort and all the equipment were left intact. It was taken over by free blacks and runaway slaves. This fort became known as Negro Fort by the whites across the border in Georgia.

As soon as General Jackson had the Red Stick Creeks sufficiently cowed and the peace (?) treaty signed, he moved with the majority of his command to Mobile. His entire command consisted of regulars; The 2nd, 3rd, 7th, 39th, and 44th Infantry Regiments plus some artillery — approximately 2500 men. Upon arriving at Mobile he took three actions which would influence the outcome of the Battle of New Orleans. He first strengthened Fort Bowyer which guarded the entrance to Mobile Bay (this is the present day site of Fort Morgan). He then wrote to Governor Blount of Tennessee asking for 2,500 militia. Next he wrote a letter to Governor Don Matteo of West Florida telling him that the Spanish must not assist the Creeks or the British in any way because that would be a breach of neutrality.

On September 15th a British force of 712 men under Colonel Nicolls, assisted by two sloops and two brigs, assaulted Fort Bowyer. They were repulsed with the loss of one ship and about 200 men. Another British force tried a land attack on Mobile but also failed. In late September Jackson received his Tennessee Volunteers, which brought his effective strength up to around five thousand men. On September 27th, Secretary of War Monroe wrote to Jackson telling him of the British threat to New Orleans and ordered him there. In October Jackson received an answer from the governor of West Florida. The reply did not satisfy Jackson regarding Spain's neutrality or her ability to control the Indians or the British. General Jackson took a force of approximately three thousand men and marched on Pensacola.

Just after Jackson left Mobile a message arrived from Washington, asking him to allow the diplomats to handle any situation relating to Spanish Florida. Even if that message had arrived before he left Mobile, it is doubtful if Jackson would have been deterred. He knew that the Spanish had only a token force in Pensacola and that the British, after having been defeated at Mobile, had very few soldiers at Fort Barrancas. In November, after a short fight, the Spaniards surrendered Pensacola to Jackson. The following day the British destroyed Fort Barrancas and escaped.

By taking Mobile and Pensacola, Jackson deprived the British of land bases close to New Orleans. In addition, it made British control of the Indians in West Florida impossible. The British had used the Indians to threaten Mobile, in hopes of tying up a large portion of Jackson's command so that he would be weakened if he did march on New Orleans. Another important aspect was that the Tennessee Volunteers were on hand for the Battle of New Orleans in December, 1814, and January, 1815. The Treaty of Ghent, which declared that a state of peace existed between the United States and England, was signed on December 24, 1814. The final battle for New Orleans took place on January 8, 1815, two weeks after the signing of the treaty. According to the book **Our Republic**, published in 1922: 'After 1815 more than thirty years passed before the throb of the war-drum was heard in the United States.'

EXTERMINATE ! ! !

exterminate   v. (L. exterminatus, fr. ex out + terminus limit) The new chemical will exterminate the cockroaches; destroy, wipe out, kill, annihilate, eliminate, eradicate, abolish, root out, erase, expunge, demolish, extinguish

'How we enjoyed ourselves in those faraway days! Those were the happy days and there was neither sin nor sorrow in the world for us. But the Clearances came upon us, destroying us all . . . turning all joy into blasphemy . . . Oh, dear man, the tears came upon my eyes when I think of all we suffered, and of the sorrows, hardships and oppressions we came through.'

> Peggy MaCormack — Speaking of being forced off her land and into ships to take her and her brethren to the new world, 1838.

'I have long viewed treaties with the Indians as an absurdity not to be reconciled to the principles of our government'

> Andrew Jackson, to President Monroe, March 1817.

During the War of 1812, Andrew Jackson spent quite a bit of time in the Alabama area as commander of the Tennessee Volunteers and the regular military. He led military expeditions against various Indian tribes in Georgia and in the Mississippi Territory. He also invaded Spanish Florida during this period. While in north Alabama, he became acquainted with the Shoals area and felt that it had great investment potential. After the War of 1812, Jackson used all his influence to have a military arsenal built and a military road constructed through that area. In 1816, in a letter to John Coffee, he mentioned that he was pressing the federal government to obtain all the land in northwest Alabama and place it on the market as soon as possible. In a letter to President Monroe, March, 1817, he again pleaded that the federal government take the northwest Alabama land from the Cherokees and sell it to white settlers. The last obstacle to white settlement in the Shoals area was removed in May, 1817, when Jackson forced Chief Doublehead of the Cherokees to cede his reserve to the federal government. Jackson was so enthusastic about forcing the Indians off their land, and being able to speculate there, that he immediately got Coffee to run surveys of several choice tracts in the Shoals area of Alabama.

The federal government announced that the sale of land in this area would be conducted during January, February and March of 1818. Jackson was very pleased at this turn of events because he thought that he would be on the scene when the sale commenced. His dreams were shattered in late December, 1817, when he received orders to take immediate command of 500 United States regulars, 1000 Tennessee militia and 2000 Creek warriors. With this personnel he was to seek out and destroy the Lower Creek Indians of Georgia and the Seminoles from Florida, who were accused by white settlers of making forays from Spanish territory into South Georgia and Alabama. Jackson joined his army in January, 1818, and prepared for his invasion of Spanish Florida.

The first battle of the First Seminole War occured about three months earlier, when in November of 1817, Chief Neamathla of Fowltown sent General Gaines (at Fort Scott) a message telling the Americans to stay out of Spanish territory. General Gaines considered this action of Chief Neamathla an impertinence and quickly dispatched Major Twiggs of Georgia with 250 men to capture the Chief. An indecisive skirmish occured as a result of this American incursion. A few days later a force of 40 men, with civilians, under the command of Lt. Richard Scott was coming up the Apalachicola River through Spanish territory. The Indians attacked them and killed 34 whites. When General Gaines was informed of this Indian attack, he requested official permission to invade Florida and punish the Seminoles. The answer from the Administration was quite vacillating. First, he was told to invade Florida, then he received word to use his own discretion in any action, next he was told that he had approval to cross into Spanish territory and attack the Seminoles; but he could not attack the Seminoles if they were near a Spanish fort. On January 4, 1818, using his own discretion, General Gaines advanced on Fowltown and burned it to the ground. He then withdrew to American territory.

In March, 1818, Jackson was ready and moved his men down the Apalachicola and captured the Spanish town of St. Marks. He then moved east to the Suwannee River where Old Town was located. This was the village of Billy Bowlegs, a Seminole Chief. The Seminoles had slipped away so all Jackson got was the Indian village, which he burned to the ground. Jackson then returned to St. Marks where he found two British citizens. He accused them of selling war material to the Indians and of instigating Indian hostility toward Americans. Even though there was no proof that these two men, Alexander Arbuthnot and Robert Ambrister, were guilty of any crime, Jackson found them guilty and had them hung. Still believing that President Monroe and Congress desired the conquest of Spanish Florida, Jackson moved his command into Pensacola and captured the capitol of West Florida. Having West Florida under his control, he ordered General Gaines to take his forces and conquer St. Augustine and East Florida.

Jackson now returned to the United States to claim the laurels as the conqueror of Spanish Florida. He was greatly surprised and shocked by the reception given him by the administration in Washington. The Monroe Administration was highly displeased with Jackson's naked aggression in Florida. Both in the House and in the Senate resolutions were introduced to censure his actions. These censure resolutions were finally voted down.

In August, 1818, President Monroe returned Florida to the Spanish authorities, but Spain, at the same time, was informed by the federal government that 'she must either govern the peninsula in a proper manner or cede to the United States a province ...' Spain realized that if she attempted to hold Florida, the United States would conquer the territory and Spain would receive no compensation. She then offered Florida to the United States for $18,000,000. The United States made counter offers and a final price of $5,000,000 was agreed upon.

On February 22, 1821, ratifications of the Adams-Onis Treaty of cession were exchanged between Spain and the United States. One clause of the treaty read:

> The inhabitants of the territories which his Catholic Majesty ceded to the United States shall be incorporated in the Union of the United States, as soon as may be consistent with the principles of the Federal Constitution, and admitted to the enjoyment of all the privileges, rights and immunities of the citizens of the United States.

In this treaty, the United States had pledged its sacred honor to the speedy granting of full citizenship to all the inhabitants of Florida; this included both the Seminoles and the free blacks.

For almost forty years the United States had been determined to get Florida, at any price. Once it was in their possession, they were going to do with it as they pleased. To the federal government, and to many Americans, the treaty with Spain was nothing but a worthless scrap of paper. Florida finally was a possession of the United States, to make or mar, and the Seminoles were in their way.

History of the 2nd Seminole War to 1837

After Florida became a territory of the U.S., the Seminoles were justly concerned about their fate. Disregarding the Adams-Onis Treaty, the United States quickly forced the Seminoles to sign a treaty. In 1823, the Treaty of Moultrie Creek (just south of St. Augustine) was signed by the Seminole Representative, Neamathla. The treaty was not wanted by the Seminole Nation, but overwhelming might forced them to sign.

The treaty gave the Seminole Nation an approximately four million acre reservation in the center of Florida. It was located between Tampa Bay and Vero Beach and the area south of Ocala. They were not allowed to be within fifteen miles of the Gulf of Mexico or the Atlantic Ocean. This treaty had a twenty year life span, guaranteed the Indians protection from any encroachment, and promised food and other necessities during the term of the treaty.

Within one year the treaty was broken by both sides.

In 1830, after Andrew Jackson became president, the Indian Removal Act was passed. It declared that equal portions of federally owned western land would be exchanged for Indian owned eastern land. This act made it legal for white settlers to displace Seminoles and force them off their land. Legislation was passed which made it illegal for an Indian to leave the reservation without a pass signed by the Indian agent; if any white settler found an Indian off the reservation, the settler could confiscate all of the Indian's belongings.

Not long after the Indian Removal Act was passed settlers from Georgia, Alabama, South Carolina and western and middle Florida began to agitate for the complete removal of all the Seminoles. On May 9, 1832 the Treaty of Paynes Landing (on the Ocklawaha River near Silver Springs) was arranged. The federal government would allow no refusal to this treaty. They threatened the Seminoles with loss of food and other harsh treatment if they did not sign. The treaty concerned removal of the Seminoles to a trans-Mississippi area in Arkansas. There was a clause which allowed Indian approval of the land. In 1833, a delegation of Seminole chiefs was taken to Fort Gibson, Arkansas Territory, to inspect the designated land. They signed the treaty which said that they approved the land. The delegation later argued that their signing only showed an approval of the land; not an agreement to remove from Florida.

The United States government had no interpreters who were knowledgeable in the Seminole tongue, nor did the Seminoles have anyone who was fluent in English. The primary interpreters were blacks who were Seminole slaves or were free men. These people did not have an in-depth knowledge of English or political interpretations. Therefore, there was quite a bit of misunderstanding on both sides.

In October, 1834, Indian Agent General Wiley Thompson began to pressure the Seminoles to leave their homeland. By 1835 the attempts to begin the removal to the trans-Mississippi area had caused a split in the Seminole Nation. There were chiefs who went along with the United States removal policy and chiefs who opposed. The increased pressure of forced removal coupled with aggravated encounters between the whites and the Seminoles over land ownership and boundaries, slaves, Indian property and other items laid the foundation for the Second Seminole War. The leaders of the anti-removal group were: Micanopy (Chief of the Seminole Nation), Jumper, Alligator, Osceola, King Philip, Wild

Cat, Sam Jones, Holatoochee and Cloud. These men were chiefs, war chiefs or sub-chiefs of the Seminoles, Mikasukis and Tallahassee.

In 1835 there were many encounters between the whites and the Indians. Hostilities came to a head during December of 1835, when war broke out in earnest. The Indians had come to the true conclusion that the white man could not be trusted. In one of their tribal meetings, possibly around Fort Brooke or Fort King, the Indians had decided to stage a general uprising and did so in late December, 1835. On December 25th, in East Florida, the Seminoles under King Philip and his son, Wild Cat, began an attack on the plantations and towns in Mosquito County. East Florida was at war. In Middle Florida, at Fort King on December 28th, Osceola and a small party attacked and killed the Indian Agent Wiley Thompson and some of his companions. Middle Florida was at war. On that same date, a relief party of 108 men under Major Dade was marching from Fort Brooke to Fort King. The Seminole chief, Alligator, with his band ambushed the United States regulars about one day from Fort King. In a short battle all but three members of the military column were killed. It would be some time before news of this ambush would reach the outside world. The Seminoles wanted to remain in Florida and would fight to do so. The Second Seminole War had started. News of the attack on Major Dade's column would reach Washington before the news of the destruction of the plantations in Mosquito County would.

The Second Seminole War was a traumatic experience for the citizens of Mosquito County and other citizens of East Florida. Many of the residents of Mosquito County were opposed to any conflict with the Indians. They had been on friendly terms with King Philip, his son, Wild Cat (Coacoochee), and their tribesmen for many years. They had eaten together, hunted together and supplied each other the necessities of life. Potter (**War in Florida**) implies this friendly relationship when he writes: 'Who is to be mainly benefited by the removal of the Indians? Is it the planter, or the farmer whose lands are already under cultivation, and who has as much as he can conveniently manage; or is it the government . . .'

Two cases showing the general feeling of the resident plantation owners toward that of hostilities with the Indians are those of John J. Bulow, of Bulowville, and George and James Anderson, of Dunn-Lawton. When Major Benjamin Putnam brought several companies of the East Florida Militia into Mosquito County in December, 1835, he first went to Bulowville. The young owner of that plantation had prepared a defensive system around his buildings and had implanted a small cannon at the entrance to the property. When Major Putnam arrived, Mr. Bulow fired this cannon at them and ordered them off his land. The militia did not take kindly to this so they forcefully took over the plantation. Major Putnam tried to impress Bulow into the militia but Bulow strongly objected to having to bear arms against his friends. For this Bulow was placed in close arrest and all his property confiscated for the use of the militia. When the militia retreated from Mosquito County a few weeks later they would not allow Bulow to take any of his personal belongings with him. Shortly after he had Bulow placed in house arrest, Putnam ordered Lt. Williams to take 10 men of Company B, 2nd Battalion, East Florida Militia (the Mosquito Roarers) to Dunn-Lawton, he found that the sugar mill area had been enclosed with a stockade and blockhouses were being erected. The Anderson brothers were preparing to defend their property from any aggressor whether that aggressor was the Indian or the white man. Williams, seeing the determination of the Andersons, quickly drew up his small detachment and in the name of the Territory of Florida and ten muskets, impressed James and George Anderson into his militia company.

Not only were the plantation owners opposed to the possibility of hostilities with their neighbors, but the Florida settler as a whole in East Florida wanted no part in fighting their friends. Dr. Motte in his book (**Journey into Wilderness**) mentions how the settlers often refused to leave their homes and to bear arms. He mentions when the local militia absolutely refused to be called to arms, another time they rose up against their own officers, and once Motte was afraid that the commanding officer of the artillery regiment he was attached to, would be killed by the local militia when he ordered them to fight. In early January of 1836, twenty-two members of the Mosquito County company petitioned Major Putnam to allow them to go home. When General Hernandez, commander of the East Florida Militia, heard of this, he realized that he was faced with the imminent desertion of a large portion of his command. To preclude the possibility of any desertion, he allowed the Mosquito County personnel to return to their home areas and watch for Indians.

In the middle of January, Major Putnam received word from Sergeant Cooper, who with five men was in the vicinity of New Smyrna, that Indians were sighted. Major Putnam immediately loaded about forty men of Company A and B into boats and departed for New

Smyrna. On the evening of January 17th, they arrived at the Dunn-Lawton plantation. He made contact with Sergeant Cooper and found that the Indians had set fire to the Anderson residence and were still in the area. His men searched the area and found that the Indians had penned some cattle near some Negro houses. Putnam placed his men near these houses knowing that the Indians should be there in the morning. About dawn two Indians approached the penned cattle and the militiamen opened fire on them. They killed one Indian and the other escaped. Putnam realized that the Indians would return in force so he withdrew his men closer to their boats. He established a defensive line and waited. They did not have long to wait before a sizeable force of

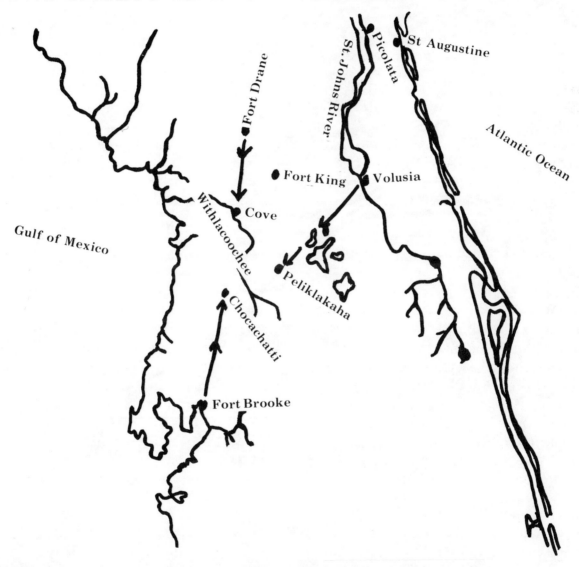

General Scott's three pronged movement to press the Seminoles into the Cove of the Withlacoochee and thus destroy their fighting strength, March - April, 1836.

Left wing under General Eustis moved from Volusia to Pelikakaha.

Center wing under Colonel Lindsey moved from Fort Brooke to Chocachatti just south of the Cove.

Right wing under General Clinch moved from Fort Drane south to the Cove.

84

Seminoles led by either King Philip or his son Wild Cat (Coacoochee) began to attack their position. This skirmishing lasted about an hour when Putnam ordered a retreat to the boats. As they were retreating and pushing their boats into the water, Lt. William H. Williams showed his disdain for the Indian marksmanship by baring his posterior toward them. He dared them to hit him, which they immediately did. The militia who saw this happen had no sympathy for Williams. In this engagement the militia's casualities were seventeen wounded and one killed. Putnam retreated posthaste for Bulowville. Hernandez, hearing of this skirmish, tried to send reinforcements to Bulowville, but the militia at St. Augustine refused to go.

Putnam then retreated to the area just south of St. Augustine so by the end of January all the country south of the outskirts of St. Augustine was deserted by the white man. The Seminole were in complete control of Mosquito County. By mid February, 1836, militia from various southern states arrived in St. Augustine and strengthened that city's defenses. Regular military forces also began to arrive during the same time.

In March, United States forces in East Florida began to gather at the trading post of Volusia in Mosquito County. This post was along the St. Johns River. The military was planning a tree-pronged attack to destroy the Seminole Indians. One army was to go from Volusia across the territory to Peliklakaha. Another unit was to leave Fort Drane (near Ocala) and move into the Indian strong hold of the Withlacoochee River. The third column was to leave Fort Brooke and move northward. During this seek and destroy mission much Indian sign was found but no Indians. The mission was a failure. During the remainder of 1836 and all 1837 until September there was little fighting in Mosquito County.

All this changed on September 4, when four Negroes, who had escaped from the Seminoles arrived at Fort Peyton (just south of St. Augustine). They reported a large concentration of Seminoles in the vicinity of Mosquito Lagoon. Three days later a detachment of 170 men left Fort Peyton and moved south for Bulowville and then for the Mosquito Lagoon area. This movement would result in the beginning of the end for Seminole power in East Florida.

That evening the detachment arrived at Bulowville and prepared camp in a heavy rain. Five escaped Negroes arrived at the military camp and one of them, John Philip, agreed to lead the military to the Seminole encampment. The next day, leaving one company to guard the Tomoka River crossing, the main body moved out. Early that evening they located the Indian camp and prepared an ambuscade. At dawn of September 9th, the Indian camp was attacked. The entire Indian force was captured except for one Indian who escaped. King Philip, the principal Seminole chief in the Mosquito Lagoon area was one of those captured. It was his son who had escaped. Among the captured Indians was one called Tomoka John. He said that he would lead the military to an encampment of Uchee Indians. That afternoon a force of one hundred men left for the Uchee Indian camp. Early the next morning the Indian camp was located and surrounded. The Indians' dogs smelled the whites and began to bark. As soon as this happened the Indians extinguished their camp fires. At dawn the Americans charged into the Uchee camp and after a hard fight captured the entire group. Among those captured was Uchee Billy,

another Seminole chief. The Americans suffered one casualty, Lt. McNeil who was mortally wounded. The Americans then withdrew to Fort Peyton, arriving there on September 1.

Now took place one of the most dastardly deeds of the Second Seminole War. After capturing Wild Cat, son of King Philip, and Blue Snake who came in under a flag of truce to find out the condition of King Philip, General Jesup decided to use this method to capture Seminoles. Around the middle of October, General Jesup received word that Osceola and Coa Hadjo were willing to meet with the whites and discuss peace. Jesup agreed to this conference and sent General Hernandez to arrange the council near Fort Peyton. Jesup planned to capture the entire Indian peace party as soon as possible. On the 20th of October, Osceola and his followers arrived near Fort Peyton. The next day Hernandez, with a force of approximately 200 men, arrived at the site of the peace conference. While a discussion was going on the American forces surrounded the Seminoles. All the Indians were captured without a fight. Hernandez marched all the Indians to St. Augustine where the inhabitants viewed the Indians as they were taken to Fort Marion.

Jesup had already made plans for the winter campaign against the Seminoles. With the capture of so many Indians, with their main chiefs, during the months of September and October 1837, his plan of attack was much easier. One wing, under Hernandez would go straight down the eastern seaboard; another wing, under Colonel Taylor would leave from Fort Brooke and move southeasterly to Lake Okeechobee; the center wing would head down the center of the territory along the St Johns River. The main purpose was to move the Indians into the southern part of the territory.

On November 6th, the Army under Hernandez left St. Augustine for New Smyrna. Arriving there the next day they established their main base camp. They stayed in New Smyrna almost the entire month of November preparing for the main campaign by laying in stores, recaulking boats and training personnel. On November 29th they left New Smyrna in Mackinaw boats and a commander's sloop. The approximately 200 military men sailed south through Mosquito Lagoon to the Haulover (near present day Titusville). One company of artillery was left at New Smyrna to protect the supplies and to guard that area from Indian attacks. When the military force landed at Haulover they met Hernandez who, with a strong force, came overland. A base camp was established at the Haulover to protect supplies as they were transferred from the Mosquito Lagoon to the Indian River to be shipped further south.

With the establishment of this advance base camp, called Fort Ann, along the east coast of Florida and the advancing American army down the center of the territory coupled with Colonel Taylor moving eastward from Fort Brooke, we have the beginning of the end of the Second Seminole War.

APPENDIX

1. Chronology of Emancipation in the United States, 1774-1810.

2. Definitive Treaty of Peace between United States of America and His Britannic Majesty, Sept. 3, 1783.

3. Treaty of Friendship, Limits, and Navigation, between United States of America and King of Spain, Oct. 27, 1795.

4. Resolution and Acts Relative to the Occupation of the Floridas by the United States of America. Secret sessions of Congress, Jan. 1811, Mar. 1811, Feb. 1813.

5. Treaty of Amity, Settlement, and Limits: Treaty ceding the Floridas from Spain to the United States, Feb. 12, 1821.

6. Acts of Acquisition and Occupation of East and West Florida, Mar. 3, 1819.

7. Act of Congress to execute the treaty between Spain and the United States, ceding Florida to the United States, Mar. 3, 1821.

8. Instructions and Commissions for Occupation of East and West Florida, Mar. 12, 1821.

9. Commission to Major General Andrew Jackson, Mar. 20, 1821.

10. Colonel Butler to the Secretary of State, regarding provisions for the Spanish military, June 20, 1821.

11. Process Verbal at St. Augustine, July 10, 1821.

12. Process Verbal at Pensacola, July 17, 1821.

13. Proclamation of Major General Andrew Jackson, July 17, 1821.

14. Ordinances of Major General Andrew Jackson, July 21, 1821.

15. Ordinance prescribing the mode of carrying into effect the 6th Article of the Treaty of Amity, July 21, 1821.

16. Supreme Court decision, Cherokee Nation v. Georgia, 1831.

17. Treaty of Moultrie Creek, with Florida Tribes of Indians, Sept. 18, 1823.

18. Treaty of Payne's Landing, with Seminoles, May 9, 1832.

19. Treaty with the Appalachicola Band, Oct. 11, 1832.

20. Removal of Southern Indians to Indian Territory, Dec. 7, 1835. (Extract from Jackson's Seventh Annual Message to Congress.)

CHRONOLOGY OF EMANCIPATION IN THE UNITED STATES 1774 to 1810

1774 Rhode Island prohibits the importation of slaves.

1776 Society of Friends in Pennsylvania requires all those of their faith to free their slaves or be expelled.

1777 Vermont Constitution forbids slavery.

1778 Virginia prohibits the importation of foreign slaves.

1780 Massachusetts Constitution says all men are free and equal by birth.

1783 Judicial decision declares that the Massachusetts clause abolished slavery in that state.

1784 Rhode Island and Connecticut pass gradual emancipation laws.

1787 Virginia cedes her Northwest Territory to the United States. One condition being that salvery be forever prohibited from that territory, but that slaves fleeing there from their owners should be returned.

1787 Constitutional convention of 1787 provides that the slave trade not be abolished until 1808. Virginia desired the immediate abolishment of that trade but was opposed by the New England States, South Carolina and Georgia.

1799 New York passes a gradual emancipation act.

1800 United States citizens barred from exporting slaves.

1804 New Jersey adopts a gradual emancipation act.

1807 United States and England prohibit any engagement in the international slave trade.

1808 United States abolishes international slave trade. The only countries with a European heritage which followed a national policy to eliminate slavery, up to the early nineteenth century, were the United States, England and France.

countries, upon the ground of reciprocal advantages and mutual convenience, as may promote and secure to both perpetual peace and harmony: And having for this desirable end, already laid the foundation of peace and reconciliation, by the provisional articles, signed at Paris, on the thirtieth of November, one thousand seven hundred and eighty-two, by the commissioners empowered on each part, which articles were agreed to be inserted in, and to constitute the treaty of peace proposed to be concluded between the crown of Great-Britain and the said United States, but which treaty was not to be concluded until terms of peace should be agreed upon between Great-Britain and France, having since been concluded, his Britannic Majesty and the United States of America, in order to carry into full effect the provisional articles abovementioned, according to the tenor thereof, have constituted and appointed, that is to say, His Britannic Majesty on his part, David Hartley, Esquire, Member of the Parliament of Great-Britain; and the said United States on their part, John Adams, Esquire, late a Commissioner of the United States of America at the Court of Versailles, late Delegate of Congress from the state of Massachusetts, and Chief of Justice of the said state, and Minister Plenipotentiary of the said United States to their High Mightinesses the States General of the United Netherlands; Benjamin Franklin, Esquire, late Delegate in Congress from the state of Pennsylvania, President of the Convention of the said state, and Minister Plenipotentiary from the United States of America at the Court of Versailles; John Jay, Esquire, late President of Congress, and Chief Justice of the state of New York, and Minister Plenipotentiary from the said United States at the Court of Madrid, to be the Plenipotentiaries for the concluding and signing the present definitive treaty; who after having reciprocally communicated their respective full powers, have agreed upon and confirmed the following articles.

ARTICLE I.

His Britannic Majesty acknowledges the said United States, viz. New-Hampshire, Massachusetts-Bay, Rhode-Island, and Providence Plantations, Connecticut, New-York, New-Jersey, Pennsylvania, Delaware, Maryland, Virginia, North-Carolina, South-Carolina, and Georgia, to be free, sovereign and independent States; that he treats with them as such; and for himself, his heirs and successors, relinquishes all claims to the government, propriety and territorial rights of the same, and every part thereof.

ARTICLE II.

And that all disputes which might arise in future, on the subject of the boundaries of the said United States, may be prevented, it is hereby agreed and declared, that the following are, and shall be their boundaries, viz. From the north-west angle of Nova-Scotia, viz. that angle which is formed by a line, drawn due north from the source of St. Croix river to the Highlands; along the said Highlands which divide those rivers, that empty themselves into the river St. Lawrence, from those which fall into the Atlantic Ocean, to the northwesternmost head of Connecticut river, thence down along the middle of that river, to the forty-fifth degree of north latitude; from thence, by a line due west on said latitude, until it strikes the river Iroquois or Cataraguy; thence along the middle of said river into lake Ontario, through the middle of said lake until it strikes the communication by water between that lake and lake Erie; thence along the middle of said communication into lake Erie, through the middle of said lake until it arrives at the water-communication between that lake and lake Huron; thence along the middle of said water-communication into the lake Huron; thence through the middle of said lake to the water-communication between that lake and lake Superior; thence through lake Superior northward of the isles Royal and Phelipeaux, to the Long Lake; thence through the middle of said Long Lake, and the water-communication between it and the Lake of the Woods, to the said Lake of the Woods; thence through the said lake to the most north-western point thereof, and from thence on a due west course to the river Mississippi; thence by a line to be drawn along the middle of said river Mississippi until it intersect the northernmost part of the thirty-first degree of northlatitude. South by a line to be drawn due east from the determination of the line last mentioned, in the latitude of thirty-one degrees north of the Equator, to the middle of the river Apalachicola or Catahouche; thence along the middle thereof to its junction with the Flint river; thence strait to the head of St. Mary's river; and thence down along the middle of St. Mary's river to the Atlantic ocean. East by a line to be drawn along the middle of the river St. Croix, from its mouth in the Bay of Fundy to its source, and from its source directly north to the aforesaid Highlands which divide the rivers that fall into the Atlantic ocean, from those which fall into the river St. Lawrence; comprehending all islands within twenty leagues of any part of the shores of the United States, and lying between lines to be drawn due east from the points where the aforesaid boundaries between Nova-Scotia on the one part, and East-Florida on the other, shall respectively touch the Bay of Fundy and the Atlantic ocean; excepting such islands as now are, or heretofore have been within the limits of the said province of Nova-Scotia.

ARTICLE III.

It is agreed that the people of the United States shall continue to enjoy unmolested the right to take fish of every kind on the Grand Bank, and on all the other banks of Newfoundland; also in the gulph of St. Lawrence, and at all other places in the sea, where the inhabitants of both countries used at any time heretofore to fish; and also that the inhabitants of the United States shall have liberty to take fish of every kind on such part of the coast of Newfoundland as British fisherman shall use (but not to dry or cure the same on that island); and also on the coasts, bays and creeks of all other of his Britannic Majesty's dominions in America; and that the American fisherman shall have liberty to dry and cure fish in any of the unsettled bays, harbours and creeks of Nova-Scotia, Magdalen islands, and Labrador, so long as the same remain unsettled, it shall not be lawful for the said fishermen to dry or cure fish at such settlement, without a previous agreement for that purpose with the inhabitants, proprietors or possessors of that ground.

ARTICLE IV.

It is agreed that creditors on either side, shall meet with no lawful impediment to the recovery of the full value in sterling money, of all bona fide debts heretofore contracted.

ARTICLE V.

It is agreed that the Congress shall earnestly recommend it to the legislatures of the respective states, to provide for the restitution of all estates, rights and properties, which have been confiscated, belonging to real British subjects, and also of the estates, rights and properties of persons resident in districts in the possession of his Majesty's arms, and who have not borne arms against the United States. And that persons of any other discription shall have free liberty to go to any part or parts of any of the thirteen United States, and therein to remain twelve months, unmolested in the endeavours to obtain the restitution of such of their estates, rights and properties, as may have been confiscated; and that Congress shall also earnestly recommend to the several states a reconsideration and revision of all acts or laws regarding the premises, so as to render the said laws or acts perfectly consistent, not only with justice and equity, but with that spirit of conciliation, which on the return of the blessings of peace should universally prevail. And that Congress shall also earnestly recommend to the several states, that the estates, rights and properties of such last mentioned persons, shall be restored to them, they refunding to any persons who may be now in possession, the bona fide price (where any has been given) which such persons may have paid on purchasing any of the said lands, rights, or properties, since the confiscation. And it is agreed, that all persons who have any interest in confiscated lands, either by debts, marriage settlements, or otherwise, shall meet with no lawful impediment in the prosecution of their just rights.

ARTICLE VI.

The there shall be no future confiscations made, nor any prosecutions commenced against any person or persons for, or by reason of the part which he or they may have taken in the present war; and that no person shall, on that account, suffer any future loss or damage, either in his person, liberty or property; and that those who may be in confinement on such charges, at the time of the ratification of the treaty in America, shall be immediately set at liberty, and the prosecutions so commenced be discontinued.

ARTICLE VII.

There shall be a firm and perpetual peace between his Britannic Majesty and the States and between the subjects of the one and the citizens of the other, wherefore all hostilities, both by sea and land, shall from henceforth cease: all prisoners on both sides shall be set at liverty, and his Britannic Majesty shall, with all convenient speed, and without causing any destruction, or carrying away any negroes or other property of the American inhabitants, withdraw all his armies, garrisons and fleets from the said United States, and from every post, place and harbour within the same; leaving in all fortifications the American artillery that may be therein; and shall also order and cause all archives, records, deeds and papers, belonging to any of the said states, or their citizens, which in the course of the war may have fallen into the hands of his officers, to be forthwith restored and delivered to the proper states and persons to whom they belong.

ARTICLE VIII.

The navigation of the river Mississippi, from its source to the ocean, shall for ever remain free and open to the subjects of Great-Britain, and the citizens of the United States.

ARTICLE IX.

In case it should so happen that any place or territory belonging to Great-Britain or to the United States, should have been conquered by the arms of either from the other, before the arrival of the said provisional articles in America, it is agreed, that the same shall be restored without difficulty, and without requiring any compensation.

ARTICLE X.

The solemn ratifications of the present treaty, expedited in good and due form, shall be exchanged between the contracting parties, in the space of six months, or sooner if possible, to be computed from the day of the signature of the present treaty. In witness whereof, we the undersigned, their Minister Plenipotentiary, have in their name and in virtue of our full powers, signed with our hands the present definitive treat, and caused the seals of our arms to be affixed thereto.

Done at Paris, this third day of September, in the year of our Lord one thousand seven hundred and eighty-three.

D. Hartley   (L.S)
John Adams   (L.S)
B. Franklin   (L.S)
John Jay   (L.S)

TREATY OF FRIENDSHIP, LIMITS AND NAVIGATION

Between the United States of America, and the King of Spain.

His Catholic Majesty· and the United States of America, desiring to consolidate, on a permanent basis, the friendship and good correspondence, which happily prevails between the two parties, have determined to establish, by a convention, several points, the settlement whereof will be productive of general advantage and reciprocal utility to both nations.

With this intention, his Catholic Majesty has appointed the most excellent Lord, don Manuel de Godoy, and Alvarez de Faria, Rios, Sanchez, Zarzosa, Prince de la Paz, duke de la Alcudia, lord of the Soto de Roma, and of the state of Albalá, Grandee of Spain of the first class, perpetual regidor of the city of Santiago, knight of the illustrious order of the Golden Fleece, and great Cross of the Royal and distinguished Spanish order of Charles the III. commander of Valencia, del Ventoso Rivera, and Acenchal in that of Santiago; Knight and Great Cross of the religious order of St. John; Counsellor of state; first Secretary of state and despacho; Secretary to the Queen; Superintendant General of the posts and highways; Protector of the royal Academy of the noble arts, and of the royal societies of natural history, botany, chemistry, and astronomy; Gentleman of the King's chamber in employment; Captain General of his armies; Inspector and Major of the royal corps of body guards, & c. & c. &c. and the President of the United States, with the advice and consent of their Senate, has appointed Thomas Pinckney, a citizen of the United States, and their Envoy Extraordinary to his Catholic Majesty. And the said Plenipotentiaries have agreed upon and concluded the following articles:

ARTICLE I.

There shall be a firm and inviolable peace and sincere friendship between his Catholic Majesty, his successors and subjects, and the United States, and their citizens, without exception of persons or places.

ARTICLE II.

To prevent all disputes on the subject of the boundaries which separate the territories of the two high contracting parties, it is hereby declared and agreed as follows, to wit: The southern boundary of the United States, which divides their territory from the Spanish colonies of East and West Florida, shall be designated by a line beginning on the river Mississippi, at the northernmost part of the thirty-first degree of latitude north of the equator, which from

thence shall be drawn due east to the middle of the river Apalachicola, or Catahouche, thence along the middle thereof to its junction with the Flint: thence straight to the head of St. Mary's river, and thence down the middle thereof to the Atlantic ocean. And it is agreed, that if there should be any troops, garrisons, or settlements of either party, in the territory of the other, according to the above-mentioned boundaries, they shall be withdrawn from the said territory within the term of six months after the ratification of this treaty, or sooner if it be possible; and that they shall be permitted to take with them all the goods and effects which they possess.

ARTICLE III.

In order to carry the preceding article into effect, one commissioner and one surveyor shall be appointed by each of the contracting parties, who shall meet at the Natchez, on the left side of the river Mississippi, before the expiration of six months from the ratification of this convention, and they shall proceed to run and mark this boundary according to the stipulation of the said article. They shall make plats and keep journals of their proceedings, which shall be considered as part of this convention, and shall have the same force as if they were inserted therein. And if on any account it should be found necessary that the said commissioners and surveyors should be accompanied by guards, they shall be furnished in equal proportions by the commanding officer of his Majesty's troops in the two Floridas, and the commanding officer of the troops of the United States in their southwestern territory, who shall act by common consent, and amicably, as well with respect to this point as to the furnishing of provisions and instruments, and making every other arrangement which may be necessary or useful for the execution of this article.

ARTICLE IV.

It is likewise agreed that the western boundary of the United States which separates them from the Spanish colony of Louisiana, is in the middle of the channel or bed of the river Mississippi, from the northern boundary of the said states to the completion of the thirty-first degree of latitude north of the equator. And his Catholic Majesty has likewise agreed that the navigation of the said river, in its whole breadth from its source to the ocean, shall be free only to his subjects and the citizens of the United States, unless he should extend this privilege to the subjects of other powers by special convention.

ARTICLE V.

The two high contracting parties shall, by all the means in their power, maintain peace and harmony among the several Indian nations who inhabit the country adjacent to the lines and rivers, which, by the preceding articles, form the boundaries of the two Floridas. And the better to obtain this effect, both parties oblige themselves expressly to restrain by force all hostilities on that part of the Indian nations living within their boundary: so that Spain will not suffer her Indians to attack the citizens of the United States, nor the Indians inhabiting their territory; nor will the United States permit these last-mentioned Indians to commence hostilities against the subjects of his Catholic Majesty or his Indians, in any manner whatever.

And whereas several treaties of friendship exist between the two contracting parties and the said nations of Indians, it is hereby agreed that in future no treaty of alliance or other whatever (except treaties of peace) shall be made by either party with the Indians living within the boundary of the other, but both parties will endeavour to make the advantages of the Indian trade common and mutually beneficial to their respective subjects and citizens, observing in all things the most complete reciprocity, so that both parties may obtain the advantages arising from a good understanding with the said nations, without being subject to the expence which they have hitherto occasioned.

ARTICLE VI.

Each party shall endeavour, by all means in their power, to protect and defend all vessels and other effects belonging to the citizens or subjects of the other, which shall be within the extent of their jurisdiction by sea or by land, and shall use all their efforts to recover and cause to be restored to the right owners, their vessels and effects which may have been taken from them within the extent of their said jurisdiction, whether they are at war or not with the power whose subjects have taken possession of the said effects.

ARTICLE VII.

And it is agreed that the subjects or citizens of each of the contracting parties, their vessels or effects, shall not be liable to any embargo or detention on the part of the other, for any military expedition or other public or private purpose whatever: And in all cases of seizure, detention, or arrest for debts contracted, or offences committed by any citizen or subject of the one party within the jurisdiction of the other, the same shall be made and prosecuted by order and authority of law only, and according to the regular course of proceedings usual in such cases. The citizens and subjects of both parties shall be allowed to employ such advocates, solicitors, notaries, agents and factors, as they may judge proper, in all their affairs, and in all their trials at law, in which they may be concerned, before the tribunals of the other party; and such agents shall have free access to be present at the proceedings in such causes, and at the taking of all examinations and evidence which may be exhibited in the said trials.

ARTICLE VIII.

In case the subjects and inhabitants of either party, with their shipping, whether public and of war, or private and of merchants, be forced, through stress of weather, pursuit of pirates or enemies, or any other urgent necessity, for seeking of shelter and harbour, to retreat and enter into any of the rivers, bays, roads or ports belonging to the other party, they shall be received and treated with all humanity, and enjoy all favor, protection and help, and they shall be permitted to refresh and provide themselves, at reasonable rates, with victuals and all things needful for the sustenance of their persons, or reparation of their ships and prosecution of their voyage; and they shall no ways be hindered from returning out of the said ports or roads, but may remove and depart when and whither they please, without any let or hindrance.

ARTICLE IX.

All ships and merchandize, of what nature soever, which shall be rescued out of the hands of any pirates or robbers on the high seas, shall be brought into some port of either state, and shall be delivered to the custody of the officers of that port, in order to be taken care of, and restored entire to the true proprietor, as soon as due and sufficient proof shall be made concerning the property thereof.

ARTICLE X.

When any vessel of either party shall be wrecked, foundered, or otherwise damaged, on the coasts or within the dominion of the other, their respective subjects or citizens shall receive, as well for themselves as for their vessel and effects, the same assistance which would be due to the inhabitants of the country where the damage happens, and shall pay the same charges and dues only as the said inhabitants would be subject to pay in a like case: And if the operations of repair would require that the whole or any part of the cargo be unladen, they shall pay no duties, charges or fees on the part which they shall relade and carry away.

ARTICLE XI.

The citizens and subjects of each party shall have power to dispose of the personal goods, within the jurisdiction of the other, by testament, conation or otherwise, and their representatives being subjects or citizens of the other party, shall succeed to their said personal goods, whether by testament or ab intestato, and they may take possession thereof, either by themselves or others acting for them, and dispose of the same at their will, paying such dues only as the inhabitants of the country wherein the said goods are, shall be subject to pay in like cases.

And in case of the absence of the representative, such care shall be taken of the said goods, as would be taken of the goods of a native in like case, until the lawful owner may take measures for receiving them. And if questions shall arise among several claimants to which of them

the said goods belong, the same shall be decided finally by the laws and judges of the land wherein the said goods are. And where, on the death of any person holding real estate within the territories of the one party, such real estate would by the laws of the land descend on a citizen or subject of the other, were he not disqualified by being an alien, such subject shall be allowed a reasonable time to sell the same, and to withdraw the proceeds without molestation, and exempt from all rights of detraction on the part of the government of the respective states.

ARTICLE XII.

The merchant-ships of either of the parties which shall be making into a port belonging to the enemy of the other party, and concerning whose voyage, and the species of goods on board her, there shall be just grounds of suspicions, shall be obligated to exhibit as well upon the high seas as in the ports and havens, not only her passports but likewise certificates, expressly showing that her goods are not of the number of those which have been prohibited as contraband.

ARTICLE XIII.

For the better promoting of commerce on both sides, it is agreed, that if a war shall break out between the said two nations, one year after the proclamation of war shall be allowed to the merchants, in the cities and towns where they shall live, for collecting and transporting their goods and merchandizes: And if any thing be taken from them or any injury be done them within that term, by either party, or the people or subjects of either, full satisfaction shall be made for the same by the government.

ARTICLE XIV.

No subject of his Catholic Majesty shall apply for, or take any commission or letters of marque, for arming any ship or ships to act as privateers against the said United States, or against the citizens, people or inhabitants of the said United States, or against the property of any of the inhabitants of any of them, from any prince or state with which the said United States shall be at war.

Nor shall any citizen, subject or inhabitant of the said United States apply for or take any commission or letters of marque for arming any ship or ships to act as privateers against the subjects of his Catholic Majesty, or the property of any of them, from any prince or state with which the said king shall be at war. And if any person of either nation shall take such commission or letters of marque, he shall be punished as a pirate.

ARTICLE XV.

It shall be lawful for all and singular the subjects of his Catholic Majesty, and the citizens, people and inhabitants of the said United States, to sail with their ships, with all manner of liberty and security, no distinction being made who are the proprietors of the merchandizes laden thereon, from any port to the places of those who now are, or hereafter shall be at enmity with his Catholic Majesty or the United States. It shall be likewise lawful for the subjects and inhabitants aforesaid, to sail with the ships and merchandizes aforementioned, and to trade with the same liberty and security from the places, ports and havens of those who are enemies of both or either party, without any opposition or disturbance whatsoever, not only directly from the places of the enemy aforementioned, to neutral places, but also from one place belonging to an enemy, to another place belonging to an enemy, whether they be under the jurisdiction of the same prince or under several; and it is hereby stipulated, that free ships shall also give freedom to goods, and that every thing shall be deemed free and exempt which shall be found on board the ships belonging to the subjects of either of the contracting parties, although the whole lading, or any part thereof, should appertain to the enemies of either: Contraband goods being always excepted. It is also agreed, that the same liberty be extended to persons who are on board a free ship, so that although they be enemies to either party, they shall not be made prisoners or taken out of that free ship, unless they are soldiers and in actual service of the enemies.

ARTICLE XVI.

This liberty of navigation and commerce shall extend to all kinds of merchandizes, excepting those only, which are distinguished by the name of contraband: And under this name of contraband or prohibited goods, shall be comprehended arms, great guns, bombs, with the fuses, and other things belong to them, cannon-ball, gunpowder, match, pikes, swords, lances, speards, halberds, mortars, petards, grenades, saltpetre, muskets, musket-ball, bucklers, helmets, breast-plates, coats of mail, and the like kind of arms, proper for arming soldiers, musket rests, belts, horses with their furniture, and all other warlike instruments whatever. These merchandizes which follows, shall not be reckoned among contraband or prohibited goods: That is to say, all sorts of cloth, and all other manufactures woven of any wool, flax, silk, cotton, or any other materials whatever; all kinds of wearing aparel, together with all species whereof they are used to be made; gold and silver, as well coined as uncoined, tin, iron, latton, copper, brass, coals; as also wheat, barley, oats, and any other kind of corn and pulse; tobacco, and likewise all manner of spices, salted and smoked flesh, salted fish, cheese and butter, beer, oils, wines, sugars, and all sorts of salts: And in general, all provisions which serve for the sustenance of life: Furthermore, all kinds of cotton, hemp, flax, tar, pitch, ropes, cables, sails, sail-cloths, anchors, and any parts of anchors, also ships' masts, planks, wood of all kind, and all other things proper either for building or repairing ships, and all other goods whatever, which have not been worked into the form of any instrument prepared for war, by land or by sea, shall not be reputed contraband, much less, such as have been already wrought and made up for any other use; all which shall be wholly reckoned among free goods: As likewise all other merchandizes in the foregoing enumeration of contraband goods: So that they may be transported and carried in the freest manner by the subjects of both parties, even to places being only excepted, as are at that time beseiged, blocked up, or invested. And except the cases in which any ship of war, or squadron shall, in consequence of storms or other accidents at sea, be under the necessity of taking the cargo of any trading vessel or vessels, in which case they may stop the said vessel or vessels, and furnish themselves with necessaries, giving a receipt, in order that the power to whom the said ship of war belongs, may pay for the articles so taken, according to the price thereof, at the port to which they may appear to have been destined by the ship's papers: and the two contracting parties engage, that the vessels shall not be detained longer than may be absolutely necessary for their said ships to supply themselves with necessaries: That they will immediatley pay the value of the receipts, and indemnify the proprietor for all losses which he may have sustained in consequence of such transaction.

ARTICLE XVII.

To the end, that all manner of dissentions and quarrels may be avoided and prevented on one side and the other, it is agreed, that in case either of the parties hereto, should be engaged in a war, the ships and vessels belonging to the subjects or people of the other party must be furnished with sea-letters or passports, expressing the name, property, and bulk of the ship, as also the name and place of habitation of the master or commander of the said ship, that it may appear thereby, that the ship really and truly belongs to the subjects of one of the parties, which passport shall be made out and granted according to the form annexed to this treaty. They shall likewise be recalled every year, that is, if the ship happens to return home within the space of a year.

It is likewise agreed, that such ships being laden, are to be provided not only with passports, as above mentioned, but also with certificates, containing the several particulars of the cargo, the place whence the ship sailed, that so it may be known whether any forbidden or contraband goods be on board the same: which certificates shall be made out by the officers of the place whence the ship sailed in the accustomed form: And if any one shall think it fit or advisable to express in the said certificates, the person to whom the goods on board belong, he may freely do so: Without which requisites they may be sent to one of the ports of the other contracting party, and

adjudged by the competent tribunal, according to what is above set forth, that all circumstances of this ommission having been well examined, they shall be adjudged to be legal prizes, unless they shall give legal satisfaction of their property by testimony entirely equivalent.

ARTICLE XVIII.

If the ships of the said subjects, people, or inhabitants, of either of the parties, shall be met with, either sailing along the coasts or on the high seas, by any ship of war of the other, or by any privateer, the said ship of war or privateer for the avoiding of any disorder, shall remain out of cannon shot, and may send their boats a-board the merchant ship, which they shall so meet with, and may enter her to number of two or three men only, to whom the master or commander of such ship or vessel shall exhibit his passports, concerning the property of the ship, made out according to the form inserted in this present treaty, and the ship when she shall have shewed such passports, shall be free and at liberty to pursue her voyage, so as it shall not be lawful to molest or give her in any manner, or force her to quit her intended course.

ARTICLE XIX.

Consuls shall be reciprocally established, with the privileges and powers which those of the most favorable nations enjoy, in the ports where their consuls reside or are permitted to be.

ARTICLE XX.

It is also agreed that the inhabitants of the territories of each party shall respectively have free access to the courts of justice of the other, and they shall be permitted to prosecute suits for the recovery of their properties, the payment of their debts, and for obtaining satisfaction for the damages which they may have sustained, whether the persons whom they may sue be subjects or citizens of the country in which they may be found, or any other persons whatsoever, who may have taken refuge therein; and the proceedings and sentences of the said courts shall be the same as if the contending parties had been subjects or citizens of the said country.

ARTICLE XXI.

In order to terminate all differences on account of the losses sustained by the citizens of the United States in consequence of their vessels and cargoes having been taken by the subjects of his Catholic Majesty, during the late war between Spain and France, it is agreed that all such cases shall be referred to the final decision of commissioners to be appointed in the following manner. His Catholic Majesty shall name one commissioner, and the President of the United States, by and with the advice and consent of their Senate, shall appoint another, and the said two commissioners shall agree on the choice of a third, or if they cannot agree so, they shall each propose one person, and of the two names so proposed, one shall be drawn by lot in the presence of the two original commissioners, and the person whose name shall be so drawn, shall be the third commissioner: and the three commissioners so appointed, shall be sworn impartially to examine and decide the claims in question, according to the merits of the several cases, and to justice, equity, and the laws of nations. The said commissioners shall meet and sit at Philadelphia: and in the case of the death, sickness, or necessary absence of any such commissioner, his place shall be supplied in the same manner as he was first appointed, and the new commissioner shall take the same oaths, and do the same duties. They shall receive all complaints and applications authorized by this article, during eighteen months from the day on which they shall assemble. They shall have power to examine all such persons as come before them on oath or affirmation, touching the complaints in question, and also to receive in evidence all written testimony, authenticated in such manner, as they shall think proper to require or admit. The award of the said commissioners, or any two of them, shall be final and conclusive, both as to the justice of the claim and the amount of the sum to be paid to the claimants; and his Catholic Majesty undertakes to cause the same to be paid in specie, without deduction, at such times and places, and under such conditions as shall be awarded by the said commissioners.

ARTICLE XXII

The two high contracting parties, hoping that the good correspondence and friendship which happily reigns between them, will be further encreased by this treaty, and that it will contribute to augment their prosperity and opulence, will in future give to their mutual commerce all the extension and favour which the advantages of both countries may require.

And in consequence of the stipulations contained in the IV. article, his Catholic Majesty will permit the citizens of the United States, for the space of three years from this time, to deposit their merchandizes and effect in the port of New-Orleans, and to export them from thence without paying any other duty than a fair price for the hire of the stores, and his Majesty promises either to continue this permission, if he finds during that time that it is not prejudicial to the interests of Spain, or if he should not gree to continue it there, he will assign to them, on another part of the banks of the Mississippi, an equivalent establishment.

ARTICLE XXIII

The present treaty shall not be in force until ratified by the contracting parties, and the ratifications shall be exchanged in six months from this time, or sooner if possible.

In witness whereof, we, the underwritten plenipotentiaries

> of his Catholic Majesty and of the United States of America, have signed this present treaty of friendship, limits, and navigation, and have thereunto affixed our seals respectively.

Done at San Lorenzo el Real, this seven and twenty day of

> October, one thousand seven hundred and ninety-five.

THOMAS PINCKNEY   (L.S)
EL PRINCIPE DE LA PAZ, (L.S)

RESOLUTION AND ACTS

Relative to the Occupation of the Floridas by The United States of America.

Resolution.

Taking into view the peculiar situation of Spain, and of her American provinces; and considering the influence which the destiny of the territory adjoining the southern border of the United States may have upon their security, tranquility, and commerce: There,

Resolved by the Senate and House of Representatives of the United States of America, in Congress assembled, That the United States, under the peculiar circumstances of the existing crisis, cannot, without serious inquietude, see any part of said territory pass into the hands of any foreign power; and that a due regard to their own safety compels them to provide, under certain contingencies, for the temporary occupation of the said territory; they, at the same time, declare that the said territory shall, in their hands, remain subject to future negotiation.

APPROVED, January 15, 1811.

******

An Act to enable the President of the United States,

> under certain contingencies, to take possession of the country lying east of the river Perdido, and south of the state of Georgia and the Mississippi territory, and for other purposes.

Be it enacted by the Senate and House of Representatives of the United States, in Congress assembled, That the President of the United States be, and he is hereby, authorized, to take possession of, and occupy, all or any part of the territory lying east of the river Perdido, and south of the state of Georgia and the Mississippi territory, in case an arrangement has been, or shall be, made with the local authority of the said territory, for delivery up the possession of the same, or any part thereof, to the United States, or in the event of an attempt to occupy the said territory, or any part thereof, by any foreign government; and he may, for the purpose of taking possession, and occupying the territory aforesaid, and in order to maintain therein the authority of the United States, employ any part of the army and navy of the United States which he may deem necessary.

SEC. 2 And be it further enacted, That one hundred thousand dollars be appropriated for defraying such expenses as the President may deem necessary for obtaining possession as aforesaid, and the security of the said territory, to be applied under the direction of the President, out of any moneys in the treasury not otherwise appropriated.

SEC. 3 And be it further enacted, That in case possession of the territory aforesaid shall be obtained by the United States, as aforesaid, that until other provision be made by Congress, the President be, and he is hereby authorized to establish within the territory aforesaid, a temporary government, and the military, civil, and judicial, powers thereof shall be vested in such person and persons, and be exercised in such manner as be may may direct, for the protection and maintenance of the inhabitants of the said territory in the full enjoyment of their liberty, property and religion.

APPROVED, January 15, 1811.

******

An Act concerning an act to enable the President of the

> United States, under certain contingencies, to take possession of the country lying east of the river Perdido, and south of the state of Georgia and the Mississippi territory, and for other purposes, and the declaration accompanying the same.

Be it enacted by the Senate and House of Representatives of the United States of America, in Congress assembled, That this act, and the act passed during the present session of Congress, entitled 'An act to enable the President of the United States, under certain contingencies, to take possession of the country lying east of the river Perdido, and south of the state of Georgia and the Mississippi territory, and for other purposes,' and the declaration accompanying the same, be not printed or published, until the end of the next session of Congress, unless directed by the President of the United States, any law or usage to the contrary notwithstanding.

APPROVED, March 3, 1811.

******

An Act authorizing the President of the United States to
> take possession of a tract of country lying south of the Mississippi territory and west of the river Perdido.

Be it enacted by the Senate and House of Representatives of the United States of America, in Congress assembled, That the President be, and he is hereby, authorized to occupy and hold all that tract of country called West Florida, which lies west of the river Perdido, not now in possession of the United States.

SEC. 2 And be it further enacted, That, for the purpose of occupying and holding the country aforesaid, and of affording protection to the inhabitants thereof, under the authority of the United States, the President may employ such parts of the military and naval force of the United States as he may deemed necessary.

SEC. 3 And be it further enacted, That for defraying the necessary expenses, twenty thousand dollars are hereby appropriated, to be paid out of any moneys in the treasury not otherwise appropriated, and to be applied for the purposes aforesaid, under the direction of the President.

APPROVED, February 12, 1813.

******

TREATY OF AMITY, SETTLEMENT AND LIMITS

******

BY THE PRESIDENT OF THE UNITED STATES
A PROCLAMATION

WHEREAS a treaty of Amity, Settlement and Limits, between the United States of America, and His Catholic Majesty, was concluded and signed between their Plenipotentiaries in this city, on the twenty-second day of February, in the year of our Lord, one thousand eight hundred and nineteen, which treaty, word for word, is as follows:

TREATY OF AMITY, SETTLEMENT AND LIMITS

Between the United States of America and His Catholic Majesty

The United States of America and his Catholic Majesty, desiring to consolidate, on a permanent basis, the friendship and good correspondence with happily prevails between the two parties, have determined to settle and terminate all their differences and pretensions, by a Treaty, which shall designate, with precision, the limits of their respective bordering territories in North America.

With this intention, the President of the United States has furnished with their full powers John Quincy Adams, Secretary of State of the United States; and his Catholic Majesty has appointed the most excellent Lord Don Luis De Onis, Gonzales, Lopez y Vara, Lord of the town of Rayaces, perpetual Regidor of the Corporation of the City of Salamanca, Knight Grand-Cross of the Royal American Order of Isabella the Catholic, decorated with the Lys of La Vendee, Knight Pensioner of the Royal and distinguished Spanish Order of Charles the Third, Member of the Supreme Assembly of the said Royal Order, of the Council of his Catholic Majesty; his Secretary, with the Exercise of Degrees, and his Envoy Extraordinary and Minister Plenipotentiary near the United States of America.

And the said Plenipotentiaries, after having exchanged their powers, have agreed upon and concluded the following articles:

ARTICLE I

There shall be a firm and inviolable peace and sincere friendship between the United States and their citizens, and his Catholic Majesty, his successors and subjects, without exception of persons or places.

ARTICLE II

His Catholic Majesty cedes to the United States, in full property and sovereignty, all the territories which belong to him, situated to the eastward of the Mississippi, known by the name of East and West Florida. The adjacent islands dependent on said provinces, all public lots and squares, vacant lands, public edifices, fortifications, barracks, and other buildings, which are not private property, archives, and documents, which relate directly to the property and sovereignty of the said provinces, are included in this article. The said archives and documents shall be left in possession of the commissaries or officers of the United States, duly authorized to receive them.

ARTICLE III

The boundary line between the two countries, west of the Mississippi, shall begin on the Gulf of Mexico, at the mouth of the river Sabine, in the sea, continuing north along the western bank of that river, to the 32d degree of latitude; thence, by a line due north, to the degree of latitude where it strikes the Rio Roxo of Nachitoches, or Red River; then following the course of the Rio Roxo westward, to the degree of longitude 100 west from London and 23 from Washington; then crossing the said Red River, and running thence, by a line due north to the river Arkansas; thence, following the course of the southern bank of the Arkansas, to its source, in latitude 42 north; and thence, by that parallel of latitude, to the South Sea, The whole being, as laid down in Melish's map of the United States, published at Philadelphia, improved to the first of January, 1818. But, if the source of the Arkansas River shall be found to fall north or south of latitude 42, then the line shall run from the said source due south or north, as the case may be, till it meets the said parallel of latitude 42, and thence, along the said parallel, to the South Sea: All the islands in the Sabine, and the said Red and Arkansas rivers, throughout the course thus described, to belong to the United States; but the use of the waters, and the navigation of the Sabine to the sea, and of said rivers Roxo and Arkansas, throughout the extent of the said boundary, on their respective banks, shall be common to the respective inhabitants of both nations.

The two high contracting parties agree to cede and renounce all their rights, claims, and pretensions, to the territories prescribed by the said line; that is to say, the United States cede to his Catholic Majesty, and renounce forever, all their rights, claims, and pretensions to the territories lying west and south of the above-described line; and, in like manner, his Catholic Majesty cedes to the said United States, all his rights, claims, and pretensions, to any territories east and north of the said line; and for himself, his heirs, and successors, renounces all claim to the said territories forever.

ARTICLE IV

To fix this line with more precision, and to place the landmarks which shall designate exactly the limits of both nations, each of the contracting parties shall appoint a Commissioner and a Surveyor, who shall meet before the termination of one year, from the date of the ratification of this treaty, at Nachitoches, on the Red River, and proceed to run and mark the said line, from the mouth of the Sabine to the Red River, and from the Red River to the river Arkansas, and to ascertain the latitude of the source of the said river Arkansas, in conformity to what is above agreed upon and stipulated, and the line of latitude 42, to the South Sea; they shall make out plans, and keep journals of their proceedings, and the result agreed upon by them shall be considered as part of this treaty, and shall have the same force as if it were inserted therein. The two governments will amicably agree respecting the necessary articles to be furnished to those persons, and also as to their respective escorts, should such be deemed necessary.

ARTICLE V

The inhabitants of the ceded territories shall be secured in the free exercise of their religion, without any restriction; and all those who may desire to remove to the Spanish dominions, shall be permitted to sell or export their effects, at any time whatever, without being subject, in either case, to duties.

ARTICLE VI

The inhabitants of the territories which his Catholic Majesty cedes to the United States, by this Treaty, shall be incorporated in the Union of the United States, as soon as may be consistent with the principles of the Federal Constitution, and admitted to the enjoyment of all the privileges, rights, and immunities, of the citizens of the United States.

ARTICLE VII

The officers and troops of his Catholic Majesty, in the territories hereby ceded by him to the United States, shall be withdrawn, and possession of the places occupied by them shall be given six months after the exchange of the ratifications of this Treaty, or sooner, if possible, by the officers of his Catholic Majesty, to the commissioners or officers of the United States, duly appointed to receive them; and the United States shall furnish the transports and escort necessary to convey the Spanish officers and troops, and their baggage, to the Havana.

ARTICLE VIII

All the grants of land made before the 24th of January, 1818, by his Catholic Majesty, or by his lawful authorities, in the said territories ceded by his Majesty to the United States, shall be ratified and confirmed to the persons in possession of the lands, to the same extent that the same grants would be valid if the territories had remained under the dominion of his Catholic Majesty. But the owners in possession of such lands, who, by reason of the recent circumstances of the Spanish nation, and the revolutions in Europe, have been prevented from fulfilling all the conditions of their grants, shall complete them within the terms limited in the same, respectfully, from the date of this treaty; in default of which, the said grants shall be null and void. All grants made since the said 24th of January, 1818, when the first proposal, on the part of his Catholic Majesty, for the cession of the Floridas, was made, are hereby declared, and agreed to be, null and void.

ARTICLE IX

The two high contracting parties, animated with the most earnest desire of conciliation, and with the object of putting an end to all the differences which have existed between them, and of confirming the good understanding which they wish to be forever maintained between them, reciprocally renounce all claims for damages or injuries which they, themselves, as well as their respective citizens and subjects, may have suffered until the time of signing this Treaty.

The renunciation of the United States will extend to all the injuries mentioned in the Convention of the 11th of August, 1802.

2. To all claims on account of prizes made by French privateers, and condemned by French consuls, within the territory and jurisdiction of Spain.

3. To all claims of indemnities on account of the suspension of the right of deposit at New Orleans, in 1802.

4. To all claims of citizens of the United States upon the government of Spain, arising from the unlawful seizures at sea, and in the ports and territories of Spain, or the Spanish colonies.

5. To all claims of citizens of the United States upon the Spanish government, statements of which, soliciting the interposition of the government of the United States, have been presented to the Department of State, or to the Minister of the United States in Spain, since the date of the Convention of 1802, and until the signature of this Treaty.

The renunciation of his Catholic Majesty extends:

1. To all the injuries mentioned in the Convention of the 11th of August, 1802.

2. To the sums which his Catholic Majesty advanced for the return of Captain Pike from the Provincias Internas.

3. To all injuries caused by the expedition of Miranda, that was fitted out and equipped at New York.

4. To all claims of Spanish subjects upon the government of the United States, arising from unlawful seizures at sea, or within the ports and territorial jurisdiction of the United States.

Finally, to all the claims of subjects of his

Catholic Majesty upon the government of the United States, in which the interposition of his Catholic Majesty's government has been solicited, before the date of this Treaty, and since the date of the Convention of 1802, or which may have been made to the Department of Foreign Affairs of his Majesty, or to his Minister in the United States.

And the high contracting parties, respectively, renounce all claim to indemnities for any of the recent events or transactions of their respective commanders and officers in the Floridas.

The United States will cause satisfaction to be made for the injuries, if any, which, by process of law, shall be established to have been suffered by the Spanish officers, and individual Spanish inhabitants, by the late operations of the American army in Florida.

ARTICLE X

The Convention entered into between the two Governments, on the 11th of August, 1802, the ratifications of which were exchanged the 21st December, 1818, is annulled.

ARTICLE XI

The United States, exeronerating Spain from all demands in future, on account of the claims of their citizens to which the renunciations herein contained extend, and considering them entirely cancelled, undertake to make satisfaction for the same, to an amount not exceeding five million dollars. To ascertain the full amount and validity of those claims, a Commission, to consist of three Commissioners, citizens of the United States, shall be appointed by the President, by and with the advice and consent of the Senate, which Commissioner shall meet at the City of Washington, and, within the space of three years from the time of their first meeting, shall receive, examine, and decide upon the amount and validity of, all the claims included within the descriptions above mentioned. The said Commissioners shall take an oath or affirmation, to be entered on the record of their proceedings, for the faithful and diligent discharge of their duties; and, in case of the death, sickness, or necessary absence, of any such Commissioner, his

place may be supplied by the appointment, as aforesaid, or by the President of the United States, during the recess of the Senate, of another Commissioner in his stead. The said Commissioners shall be authorized to hear and examine on oath, every question relative to the said claims, and to receive all suitable authentic testimony concerning the same. And the Spanish government shall furnish all such documents and elucidations as may be in their possession, for the adjustment of the said claims, according to the principles of justice, the laws of the nations, and the stipulations of the Treaty, between the two parties, of 27th, October, 1795; the said documents to be specified, when demanded, at the instance of the said Commissioners.

The payment of such claims as may be admitted and adjusted by the said Commissioners, or the major part of them, to an amount not exceeding five millions of dollars, shall be made by the United States, either immediately at their Treasury, or by the creation of stock bearing an interest of six per cent. per annum, payable from the proceeds of sale of public lands within the Territories hereby ceded to the United States, or in such other manner as the Congress of the United States may prescribe by law.

The records of the Proceedings of the said Commissioners, together with the vouchers and documents produced before them, relative to the claims to be adjusted and decided upon by them, shall, after the close of their transactions, be deposited in the Department of State of the United States; and copies of them, or any part of them, shall be furnished to the Spanish government, if required, at the demand of the Spanish Minister in the United States.

ARTICLE XII

The Treaty of limits and navigation, of 1795, remains confirmed in all, and each one of its articles, excepting the 2, 3, 4, 21, and the second clause of the 22d article, which, having been altered by this Treaty, or having received their entire execution, are no longer valid.

With respect to the 15th article of the same Treaty of Friendship, Limits, and Navigation, of 1795, in which it is stipulated that the flag shall cover the property, the two high contracting parties agree that this shall be so understood with respect to those powers who recognize this principle; but, if either of the two contracting parties shall be at war with a third party, and the other neutral, the flag of the neutral shall cover the property of enemies whose government acknowledges this principle, and not of others.

ARTICLE XIII

Both contracting parties, wishing to favor their mutual commerce, by affording in their ports every necessary assistance to their respective merchant vessels, have agreed, that the sailors who shall desert from their vessels in the ports of the other, shall be arrested and delivered up, at the instance of the consul, who shall prove, nevertheless, that the deserters belonged to the vessels that claim them, exhibiting the document that is customary in their nation; that is to say, the American consul in a Spanish port, shall exhibit the document known by the name of articles; and the Spanish consul in American ports, the roll of the vessel; and if the name of the deserter or deserters, who are claimed, shall appear in the one or the other, they shall be arrested, held in custody, and delivered to the vessel to which they shall belong.

ARTICLE XIV

The United States hereby certify that they have not received any compensation from France, for the injuries they suffered from her privateers, consuls, and tribunals on the coasts and in the ports of Spain, for the satisfaction of which provision is made by this Treaty; and they will present an authentic statement of the prizes made, and of their true value, that Spain may avail herself of the same, in such manner as she may deem just and proper.

ARTICLE XV

The United States, to give to his Catholic Majesty a proof of their desire to cement the relations of amity subsisting between the two nations, and to favor the commerce of the subjects of his Catholic Majesty, agree that Spanish vessels, coming laden only with productions of Spanish growth or manufacture, directly from the ports of Spain, or of her colonies, shall be admitted, for the term of twelve years, to the ports of Pensacola and St. Augustine, in the Floridas, without paying other or higher duties on their cargos, or of tonnage, than will be paid by the vessels of the United States. During the said term, no other nation shall enjoy the same privileges within the ceded Territories. The twelve years shall commence three months after the exchange of the ratifications of this Treaty.

ARTICLE XVI

The present Treaty shall be ratified in due form, by the contracting parties, and the ratifications shall be exchanged in six months from this time, or sooner, if possible.

In witness whereof, we, the underwritten Plenipotentiaries

> of the United States of America and of his Catholic Majesty, have signed, by virtue of our powers, the present Treat of Amity, Settlement, and Limits, and have thereunto affixed our seals, respectively.

Done at Washington, this twenty-second day of February,

> one thousand eight hundred and nineteen.

JOHN QUINCY ADAMS (L.S.)
LUIS DE ONIS (L.S.)

And whereas his said Catholic Majesty did, on the twenty-fourth day of October, in the year of our Lord one thousand eight hundred and twenty, ratify and confirm the said treaty, which ratification is in the words and of the tenor following:

'Ferdinand the Seventh, by the Grace of God, and by the Constitution of the Spanish monarchy, king of the Spains.

'Whereas, on the twenty-second day of February, of the year one thousand eight hundred and nineteen last past, a treaty was concluded, and signed in the City of Washington, between Don Luis de Onis, my Envoy Extraordinary and Minister Plenipotentiary, and John Quincy Adams, Esquire, Secretary of State of the United States of America, competently authorized by both parties, consisting of sixteen articles, which had for their object the arrangement of differences and of limits between both governments and their respective territories; which are of the following form and literal tenor:

(Here follows the above Treaty, word for word.)

'Therefore, having seen and examined the sixteen articles aforesaid, and having first obtained the consent and authority of the General Cortes of the nation with respect to the cession mentioned and stipulated in the 2d and 3d articles, I approve and ratify all and every one of the articles referred to, and the clauses which are contained in them; and in virtue of these presents, I approve and ratify them; promising, on the faith and word of a King, to execute and observe them, and cause them to be executed and observed entirely as if I myself had signed them: and that the circumstance of having exceeded the term of six months, fixed for the exchange of the ratifications in the 16th article may afford no obstacle in any manner, it is my deliberate will that the present ratification be as valid and firm, and produce the same effect, as if it had been done within the determined period. Desirous at the same time of avoiding any doubt or ambiguity concerning the meaning of the 8th article of the said treaty, in respect to the date which is pointed out in it as the period for the confirmation of the grants of lands in the Floridas, made by me, or by the competent authorities in my royal name, which point of date was fixed in the positive understanding of the three grants of land made in favor of the Duke of Alagon, the Count of Punonrostro, and Don Pedro de Vargas, being annulled by its tenor, I think proper to declare that the said three grants have remained and do remain entirely annulled and invalid; and that neither the three individuals mentioned, nor those who may have title or interests through them, can avail themselves of the said grants at any time, or in any manner: under which explicit declaration the said 8th article is to be understood as ratified. In the faith of all which I have commanded to despatch these presents.

Signed by my hand, sealed with my secret seal, and countersigned by the underwritten my Secretary of Despatch of State.

'Given at Madrid, the twenty-fourth of October, one thousand eight hundred and twenty.

(Signed)   FERNANDO.
(Countersigned) Evaristo Perez de Castro'

And whereas the Senate of the United States did, on the nineteenth day of the present month, advise and consent to the ratification, on the part of these United States, of the said treaty, in the following words.

In Senate of the United States,
February 19th, 1821.

'Resolved, two thirds of the Senators present concurring therein, That the Senate, having examined the treaty of Amity, Settlement, and Limits, between the United States of America, and his Catholic Majesty, made and concluded on the twenty second of February, one thousand eight hundred and nineteen, and seen and considered the ratification thereof made by his Catholic Majesty, on the twenty fourth day of October, one thousand eight hundred and twenty, do consent to, and advise the President of the United States to ratify the same.'

And whereas in pursuance of the said advice and consent of the senate of the United States, I have ratified and confirmed the said Treaty, in the words following, viz;

'Now, therefore, I, James Monroe, President of the United States of America, having seen and considered the treaty above recited, together with the ratification of his Catholic Majesty thereof, do in pursuance of the aforesaid advice and consent of the Senate of the United States by these presents, accept, ratify, and confirm the said treaty, and every clause and article thereof, as the same are herein before set forth.

In faith whereof, I have caused the seal of the United States of America to be hereunto affixed.

Given under my hand, at the City of Washington, this twenty-second day of February, in the year of our Lord, one thousand eight hundred and twenty-one, and of the Independence of the United

States, the forty-fifth.

JAMES MONROE

By the President:
John Quincy Adams
Secretary of State

And whereas the said ratifications, on the part of the United States, and of his Catholic Majesty, have been this day, duly exchanged, at Washington, by John Quincy Adams, Secretary of State of the United States, and by General Don Francisco Dionisio Vives, Envoy Extraordinary, and Minister Plenipotentiary of his Catholic Majesty: Now therefore, to the end that the said treaty may be observed and performed with good faith, on the part of the United States, I have caused the premises to be made public; and I do hereby enjoin and require all persons bearing office, civil or military, within the United States, and all others, citizens or inhabitants thereof, or being within the same, faithfully to observe and fulfil the said treaty, and every clause and article thereof.

In testimony whereof, I have caused the seal of the United States to be affixed to these presents, and signed the same with my hand.

Done at the city of Washington, the twenty-second of February, in the year of our Lord one thousand eight hundred and twenty-one, and of the Sovereignty and Independence of the United States the forty-fifth.

JAMES MONROE

By the President:
John Quincy Adams
Secretary of State.'

ACTS OF ACQUISITION AND OCCUPATION EAST AND WEST FLORIDA

******

ACT OF CONGRESS, MARCH 3, 1819

An Act to authorize the President of the
United States to
take possession of East and West
Florida, and establish a temporary government therein.

Be it enacted by the Senate and House of Representatives of the United States of America, in Congress assembled, That the President of the United States be, and he is hereby, authorized to take possession of, and occupy, the territories of East and West Florida, and the appendages and appurtenances thereof; and to remove and transport the officers and soldiers of the king of Spain, being there, to the Havana, agreeably to the stipulations of a treaty between the United States, and Spain, executed at Washington, on the twenty-second day of February, in the year one thousand eight hundred and nineteen, providing for the cession of said territories to the United States; and he may, for these purposes, and in order to maintain in said territories the authority of the United States, employ any part of the army and navy of the United States, and the militia of any state or territory which he may deem necessary.

SEC. 2. And it be further enacted, That, until the end of the first session of the next Congress, unless provision for the temporary government of said territories be sooner made by Congress, all the military, civil, and judicial, powers, exercised by the officers of the existing government of the same territories, shall be vested in such person and persons, and shall be exercised in such manner, as the President of the United States shall direct, for the maintaining the inhabitants of said territories in the free enjoyment of their liberty, property, and religion; and the laws of the United States, relative to the collection of revenue, and the importation of persons of colour, shall be extended to the said territories; and the President of the United States shall be, and he is hereby, authorized, within the term aforesaid, to establish such districts, for the collection of the revenue, and, during the recess of Congress, to appoint such officers, whose commissions shall expire at the end of the next session of Congress, to enforce the said laws, as to him shall seem expedient.

SEC.3. And it be further enacted, That, the sum of twenty thousand dollars is hereby appropriated for the purpose of carrying this act into effect, to be paid out of any moneys in the treasury not otherwise appropriated, and to be applied under the direction of the President of the United States.

SEC. 4. And it be further enacted, That this act shall take effect, and be in force, whenever the aforesaid treaty, providing for the cession of said territories to the United States, shall have been ratified by the king of Spain shall be ready to surrender said territory to the United States, according to the provisions of said treaty.

******

ACT OF CONGRESS, MARCH 3, 1821

An act for carrying into execution the Treaty between the
> United States and Spain, concluded at Washington on the twenty-second day of February, one thousand eight hundred and nineteen.

Be it enacted by the Senate and House of Representatives of the United States of America, in Congress assembled, That the President of the United States be, and he is hereby, authorized to take possession of, and occupy, the Territories of East and West Florida, and the appendages and appurtenances thereof; and to remove and transport the officers and soldiers of the king of Spain, being there, to the Havanna, agreeably to the stipulations of the treaty between the United States and Spain, concluded at Washington, on the twenty-second day of February, in the year one thousand eight hundred and nineteen, providing for the cession of said territories to the United States; and he may, for these purposes, and in order to maintain in said territories the authority of the United States, employ any part of the army and navy of the United States, and the militia of any state or territory, which he may deem necessary.

Sec. 2. And it be further enacted, That, until the end of the first session of the next Congress, unless provision for the temporary government of said territories be sooner made by Congress, all the military, civil and judicial, powers exercised by the officers of the existing government of the same territories, shall be vested in such person and persons, and shall be exercised in such manner, as the President of the United (States) shall direct, for the maintaining the inhabitants of said territories in the free enjoyment of their liberty, property, and religion; and the laws of the United States relating to the revenue and its collection, subject to the modification stipulated by the fifteenth article of the said treaty, in favour of Spanish vessels and their cargoes, and the laws relating to the importation of persons of colour, shall be extended to the said territories. And the President of the United States shall be, and he is hereby, authorized within the term aforesaid, to establish such districts for the collection of the revenue, and during the recess of Congress, to appoint such officers, whose commissions shall expire at the end of the next session of Congress, to enforce the said laws, as to him shall seem expedient.

Sec. 3. And it be further enacted, That the President of the United States be, and he is hereby, authorized to appoint, during the recess of the Senate, a commissioner and surveyor, whose commissions shall expire at the end of the next session of Congress, to meet the commissioner and surveyor who may be appointed on the part of Spain, for the purposes stipulated in the fourth article of said treaty; and that the President be, and he is hereby, further authorized to take all other measures which he shall judge proper, for carrying into effect the stipulations of the said fourth article.

Sec. 4. And be it further enacted, That aboard of three commissioners shall be appointed, conformably to the stipulations of the eleventh article of the said treaty: and the President of the United States is hereby authorized to take any measures which he may deem expedient for organizing the said board of commissioners, and, for this purpose, may appoint a secretary well versed in the French and Spanish languages, and a clerk; which appointments if made during the recess of the Senate, shall, at the next meeting of that body, be subject to nomination for their advice and consent.

Sec. 5. And be it further enacted, That the compensation of the respective officers, for whose appointments provision is made by this act, shall not exceed the following sums:

The commissioner to be appointed conformably to the fourth article, at the rate, by the year, of three thousand dollars.

To the surveyor, two thousand dollars.

To each of the three commissioners to be appointed conformably to the eleventh article of the treaty, three thousand dollars.

To the secretary of the board, two thousand dollars.

To the one clerk, one thousand five hundred dollars.

Sec. 6. And it be further enacted, That, for carrying this act into execution, the sum of one hundred thousand dollars be, and hereby is, appropriated, to be taken from any moneys in the treasury not otherwise appropriated.

INSTRUCTIONS AND COMMISSIONS

FOR OCCUPATION OF EAST AND WEST FLORIDA

THE SECRETARY OF STATE

TO MAJOR GENERAL ANDREW JACKSON

Department of State, Washington, March 12, 1821.

Sir:

By direction of the President of the United States, I have the honor of transmitting to you three commissions:

1. As commissioner to receive possession of the provinces of East and West Florida, conformably to the treaty between the United States and Spain, concluded on the 22d of February, 1819.

2. As governor of the whole territories of which possession is to be thus taken.

3. As commissioner vested with special and extraordinary powers, conformably to the stipulations of the treaty, and to the act of Congress for carrying the same into execution; copies of both of which are also among the enclosures with this letter.

Together with the Spanish ratification of the treaty, there was transmitted to the Spanish minister at this place a royal order to the Captain General and Governor of the island of Cuba for delivering possession of the provinces of East and West Florida, according to the stipulations of the second article of the treaty.

Colonel James G. Forbes has been appointed by the President agent and commissary to deliver this royal order to the Governor of Cuba, to concert and arrange with him the execution of it, and to receive any documents or archives which may be at the Havana, and which are stipulated to be delivered by this article. A copy of his instructions is herewith enclosed, by which you will perceive that he is to deliver over to you all such documents or archives as he may receive at the Havana. It is desirable that those relating to each of the two provinces should be kept distinct from each other, and that this Government should be informed generally of their character and quantity.

Colonel Forbes is to take passage at New York in the United States sloop of war Hornet, Captain Read, and, on arriving at Pensacola, is to give you immediate notice, that you may repair thither to receive possession of that place. The Hornet is to remain there to escort the transport in which the Spanish officers and troops and their baggage are to be conveyed to the Havana.

The Spanish minister has expressed a strong wish that no troops of the United States may be introduced into Pensacola or St. Augustine until after the evacuation by those of Spain. The object of this request being to avoid any possible unpleasant altercations between the soldiers of the two nations, the President thinks it reasonable to comply with it, unless you should be of opinion that it will be attended with inconvenience. In that event, he relies that you will take every measure of precaution which may be necessary to guard against any such collisions between the soldiers; and he trusts with confidence that, in every arrangement for the evacuation, the utmost delicacy will be observed to avoid every thing which might tend to wound the feelings of any of the Spanish officers, soldiers or subjects who are to remove.

It is the President's desire that you should appoint General Gaines, or such other officer as you may deem expedient, to receive possession of St. Augustine; and that the same instructions should be applied to the execution of that service. The United States brig Enterprise or schooner Porpoise will be ordered to proceed to that place to escort the transports which are to convey the Spanish officers and troops thence to the Havana. The care of providing the transports at both places is referred to you. The number of troops at either place is not known, but supposed to amount to about five hundred men at each. The stipulation is understood to include civil as well as military officers, and provisions as well as passage.

Instructions will be given by the Secretary of War to the quartermaster and commissaries to furnish to your orders provisions and transports for the conveyance of the Spanish officers and troops. It is expected they will be supplied at New Orleans and Mobile for those to embark within the Gulf, and at Savannah and Charleston for those going from St. Augustine.

A copy and translation of the royal order to the Governor of Cuba, for delivering the possession of the provinces, is among the enclosures herewith. You will observe that it includes expressly the islands appurtenant to them. It will be proper that attention should be paid to taking possession of all these islands, but it may not be necessary that a formal delivery of them in every case should be made.

On receiving from the Governors of West and of East Florida possession of those respective provinces, it will be proper to exchange certificates of the time and mode of the transaction. Orders for the delivery of any military posts within the provinces will be expected, and they will be occupied by detachments of our troops, as you may deem expedient.

As soon as the possession shall be transferred, you will, in pursuance of your authority over the ceded territories issue proclamations announcing the fact. A form adapted from that which was issued on the first occupation of Louisiana is herewith enclosed, to be modified as the circumstances, in your opinion, may require.

The powers vested in you by the enclosed commissions are also conformable to those which were intrusted to the Governor of Louisiana under an act of Congress of similar import. The President is satisfied that they will be exercised by you with a due regard as well to the privileges and usages of the inhabitants under the Government to which they have been subject, as to the

personal and social rights to which they will be entitled by the stipulation of the treaty, and as associates to the union of these States. The money paid into the Spanish treasury before the delivery of possession, and whatever may be due thereto at that date, is to be considered as the property of Spain. Payments and debts subsequent to that date will belong, of course, to the United States.

The laws of the United States relating to the introduction of persons of color, being extended by the act of Congress to the territory, the execution of them will be superintendent by officers to be appointed for the several collection districts to be established by the President conformably to the law.

Your compensation as governor will be at the rate of five thousand dollars a year. As commissioner for receiving possession of the provinces, such reasonable expenses as may be incurred will be allowed. Whenever your military command ceases, your salary as governor will commence.

In the taking of possession of St. Augustine and East Florida, similar proceedings to those relative to the occupation of West Florida will be proper. Both provinces being placed under your direction, the proclamation to be issued there will be in your name; and General Gaines, or such other officer as you may appoint, will be instructed to consider himself, for all the purposes of the Government, subject to your orders.

At the ensuing session of Congress it is to be presumed one of the earliest objects of attention to that body will be to make further provision for the government of these territories. The President wishes you, in the interval, to collect and communicate to this Department any information relating to the country and its inhabitants which may be useful to the exercise of the legislative authority of the union concerning them.

For the expenses incident to the services herewith required, you will draw upon this Department. Strict economy is to be observed in incurring them; and I have urgently to request the transmission, as early as possible, of all the accounts resulting from them, with the vouchers necessary for their settlement at the Treasury.

> I am, with great respect, & c.
> John Quincy Adams.

COMMISSIONS

TO MAJOR GENERAL ANDREW JACKSON

1.

James Monroe, President of the United States of America.

To all to whom these presents shall come, Greeting:

Know Ye, That reposing special Trust and Confidence in the Patriotism and Abilities of Major General Andrew Jackson of Tennessee, I have appointed him Commissioner of the United States with full power and authority to him to take possession of and occupy the territories ceded by Spain to the United States, by the Treaty concluded at Washington on the twenty second day of February, in the year one thousand eight hundred and nineteen, and for that purpose to repair to the said Territories and there to execute and perform all such acts and things touching the premises as may be necessary for fulfilling his appointment conformable to the said Treaty and the laws of the United States: and I do moreover authorize the said Andrew Jackson to appoint any person or persons in his stead to receive possession of any part of the said ceded Territories, according to the stipulations of the said Treaty.

(Seal)

> In Testimony whereof, I have caused these Letters to be made patent, and the Seal of the United States to be hereunto affixed. Given under my hand at the City of Washington the tenth day of March, A.D. 1821; and of the Independence of the United States of America, the Forty Fifth.

> James Monroe

By the President,
> John Quincy Adams
> Secretary of State.

2.

James Monroe, President of the United States of America,

To all to whom these presents shall come, Greeting:

Whereas the Congress of the United States by An Act passed on the third day of the present month did provide that until the end of the first Session of the next Congress, unless provision be sooner made for the temporary Government of the Territories of East and West Florida, ceded by Spain to the United States, by the Treaty between the said Parties concluded at Washington on the twenty second day of February, one thousand eight hundred and nineteen, all the military civil and judicial powers exercised by the officers of the existing government of the same, shall be vested in such person and persons, and shall be exercised in such manner as the President of the United States shall direct, for maintaining the inhabitants of said Territories in the free enjoyment of their liberty, property and religion. Now Know Ye, that reposing special Trust and Confidence in the Integrity, Patriotism and Abilities of Major General Andrew Jackson, I do in virtue of the above recited Act appoint him to exercise within the said ceded Territories under such limitations as have been or may hereafter be prescribed to him by my instructions, and by law, all the powers and authorities heretofore exercised by the Governor and Captain General and Intendant of Cuba, and by the Governors of East and West Florida within the said provinces respectively; and do authorize and empower him the said Andrew Jackson to execute and fulfil the duties of this present appointment according to law; and to Have and to Hold the same with all its powers and privileges until the end of the next Session of Congress unless provision be sooner made for the temporary government of the said Territories so ceded by Spain to the United States; Provided however and it is the true intent and meaning of these presents that the said Andrew Jackson or any person acting under him or in the said territories shall have no power or authority to lay or collect any new or additional taxes or grant grant or confirm to any person or persons whomsoever any title or claims to lands within the same.

(Seal)

> In Testimony whereof, I have caused these Letters to be made patent, and the Seal of the United States to be hereunto affixed. Given under my hand at the City of Washington the tenth day of March, A.D. 1821; and of the Independence of the United States of America, the Forty Fifth.
>
> James Monroe

By the President,
    John Quincy Adams
       Secretary of State.

3.

James Monroe, President of the United States of America,

To Andrew Jackson, Greeting.

Whereas by An Act of Congress passed on the third day of the present month entitled, 'An Act for carrying into execution the Treaty between the United States and Spain, concluded at Washington on the twenty-second day of February, one thousand eight hundred and nineteen,' it is provided that until the end of the first Session of the next Congress, unless provision be sooner made for the temporary Government of the Territories ceded by Spain to the United States by the Treaty concluded at Washington on the twenty-second day of February, one thousand eight hundred and nineteen between the two Nations, all the Military Civil and judicial powers exercised by the officers of the existing Government of the same shall be vested in such person or persons, and shall be exercised in such manner as the President of the United States shall direct for maintaining the Inhabitants of said Territories in the free enjoyment of their liberty, property and religion; and Whereas on the tenth day of the present month, I did by letters patent under the Seal of the United States in pursuance of the powers vested in me as aforesaid appoint you the said Andrew Jackson to exercise under certain limitations within the said ceded Territories all the powers and authorities heretofore exercised by the Governor and Captain General and by the Intendant of Cuba, and by the Governors of East and West Florida within the said Provinces respectively, with the clauses and conditions in the said Letters patent expressed; and Whereas it appears to me expedient that you should be vested with the other powers hereinafter specified: Therefore be it known that in virtue of the above recited Act of Congress I do by these presents appoint and authorize you the said Andrew Jackson to administer the government with the existing authorities in the best manner in your power for the present, and to report without delay, the actual state, with such altercations as you may think advisable, that further instructions may be given respecting the same: and I do moreover authorize you to suspend any officer or officers in the said Territories which the public good may seem to you to require, with the exception always of such as are or may be appointed by the President of the United States, making a report to this government of your proceedings therein: these Letters patent are to continue in force until the end of the first Session of the next Congress, unless provision be sooner made for the temporary Government of the said Territories so as aforesaid ceded by Spain to the United States, and unless it should be sooner revoked by the President of the United States.

(Seal)

> In Testimony whereof, I have caused these Letters to be made patent, and the Seal of the United States to be hereunto affixed. Given under my hand at the City of Washington the twentieth day of March A.D. 1821; and of the Independence of the United States of America, the Forty Fifth.
>
> James Monroe

By the President,
    John Quincy Adams
       Secretary of State.

******

COLONEL BUTLER TO
THE SECRETARY OF STATE

St. Augustine, June 20, 1821.

Sir;

I have the honor to report to you that the understanding which at present exists between the governor who is the commissioner on the part of Spain, and myself, is, that the exchange of flags will be effected on or about the 1st of July, and in a manner which, I trust, will be deemed satisfactory by my Government.

I shall avail myself of the earliest opportunity after that event to give you in detail the whole of the proceedings on that subject.

I was induced to believe, from information received some time since, that the provision destined to subsist the Spanish forces to the Havana had arrived at Amelia island, and I therefore gave an order for their delivery to the officer commanding the detachment destined to occupy the fortress at this place. A partial supply only was delivered, and that out of the supply for the troops at that place. I have therefore despatched a transport to Amelia to procure the supply necessary, and, if not in store, to purchase such as may be wanting. I am without any advices from the commissary general's department on this subject.

I have the honor to be, very respectfully, your most obedient servant,

Robert Butler

The Hon. John Quincy Adams,
Secretary of State.

PROCESS VERBAL AT
ST. AUGUSTINE

In the place of St. Augustine, and on the 10th day of July, eighteen hundred and twenty-one, Don Jose Coppinger, colonel of the National Armies, and commissioner appointed by his Excellency the Captain General of the Island of Cuba, to make a formal delivery of his said place and province of East-Florida, to the government of the United States of America, by virtue of the treaty of cession concluded at Washington, on the twenty-second of February, eighteen hundred and nineteen,

and the royal schedule of delivery of the twenty-fourth of October of the last year, annexed to the documents mentioned in the certificate that form a heading to these instruments in testimony thereof. And the adjutant general of the southern division of said states colonel Robert Butler, duly authorized by the aforesaid government to receive the same, we having had several conferences in order to carry into effect our respective commissions, as will appear by our official communications-and having received through officers nominated by the later, the documents, inventories and plans, appertaining to the property and sovereignty of the Spanish nation held in this province, and in its adjacent Islands depending thereon, with the sites, public squares, vacant lands, public edifices, fortifications, and other works not being private property; and the same having been preceded by the arrangements and formalities, that for the greater solemnity of this important act, they have judged proper, there has been verified at 4 o'clock of the evening of this day the complete and personal delivery of the fortifications, and all else of this aforesaid province, to the commissioner, officers and troops of the United States, and in consequence thereof, having embarked for the Havana, the military and civil officers and Spanish troops in the American transports provided for this purpose, the Spanish authorities having this moment ceased the exercise of their functions, and those appointed by the American government having begun theirs- duly noting, that we have transmitted to our governments, the doubt occurring whether the artillery ought to be comprehended in the fortifications, and if the public archives relating to private property ought to remain, and be delivered to the American government by virtue of the cession: and that there remain in the fortifications, until the aforesaid resolution is made, the artillery, munitions and implements, specified in a particular inventory, awaiting on these points and the others appearing in question in our correspondence, the superior decision of our respective governments and which is to have, whatever may be the result, the most religious compliance at any time that it may arrive, and in which the possession that at present appears given, shall not serve as an obstacle. In testimony of which, and that they may at all times serve as an expressive and formal receipt in this act, we the subscribing commissioners, sign four instruments of this same tenor in the English and Spanish languages, at the above mentioned place, and said day, month and year.

(Signed) JOSE COPPINGER.
(Signed) ROBERT BUTLER.

I do hereby certify and attest that the foregoing act was solemnized in the presence of the illustrious assembly, as well as of a number of private individuals convened on the occasion, and of several officers of the army and navy of the United States.

(Signed) JUAN DE ENTRALGO
Gov't Scribe and
Secretary of the City Council.

PROCESS VERBAL AT PENSACOLA

The undersigned, Major General Andrew Jackson, of the State of Tennessee, Commissioner of the United States, in pursuance of the full powers received by him from James Monroe, President of the United States of America, of the date of the 10th of March, 1821, and of the forty-fifth of the Independence of the United States of America, attested by John Quincy Adams, Secretary of State; and Don Jose Callava, Commandant of the Province of West Florida, and Commissioner for the delivery, in the name of His Catholic Majesty, of the country, territory and dependencies of West Florida, to the Commissioner of the United States, in conformity with the powers, commission and special mandate received by him from the Captain General of the Island of Cuba, of the date of the fifth of May, 1821, imparting to him therein the royal order of the 24th of October, 1820, issued and signed by His Catholic Majesty Ferdinand VII, and attested by the Secretary of State, Don Evaristo Perez de Castro:

Do certify by these presents, that on the seventeenth day of July, 1821, of the Christian era, and forty-sixth of the Independence of the United States, having met in the court room of the government house in the town of Pensacola, accompanied on either part by the chiefs and officers of the army and navy, and by a number of the citizens of the respective nations, and said Andrew Jackson, Major General and Commissioner, has delivered to the said Colonel Commandant Don Jose Callava, his before-mentioned powers, whereby he recognizes him to have received full power and authority to take possession of and to occupy the territories ceded by Spain to the United States, by the Treaty concluded at Washington on the 22d day of February, 1819, and for that purpose to repair to said territories, and there to execute and perform all such acts and things touching the premises as may be necessary for fulfilling his appointment conformably to the said treaty and the laws of the United States-with authority likewise to appoint any person or persons in his stead to receive possession of any part of the said ceded territories according to the stipulations of the said treaty; whereupon the Colonel Commandant, Don Jose Callava immediately declared that in virtue and in performance of the power, commission & special mandate dated at Havana on the 5th of May 1821, be thenceforth and from that moment placed the said commissioner of the United States in possession of the country, territories and dependencies of West Florida including the fortress of St. Marks, with the adjacent islands dependent upon said province, all public lots and squares, vacant lands, public edifices, fortifications, barracks and other buildings which are not private property according to the manner set forth in the inventories and schedules which he has signed and delivered with the archives and documents directly relating to the property and sovereignty of the said Territory of West Florida, including the fortress of St. Marks, and situated to the east of the Mississippi river, the whole in conformity with the second article of the treaty of cession; concluded at Washington the twenty-second of February, 1819, between Spain and the United States, by

Don Louis de Onis, Minister Plenipotentiary of his Catholic Majesty, and John Quincy Adams, Secretary of State of the United States, both provided with full powers, which treaty has been ratified on the part of his Catholic Majesty Ferdinand the seventh, on the one part, and the President of the United States on the other part; which ratifications have been duly received and exchanged at Washington, the twenty-second of February, 1821, and the forth-fifth of the Independence of the United States of America, by General Don Dyonisius Vives, Minister Plenipotentiary of his Catholic Majesty, and John Quincy Adams, Secretary of the United States, according to the instrument signed on the same day.

And the present delivery of the country is made in order, that in the execution of the said treaty, the sovereignty and the property of that province of West Florida, including the fortress of St. Marks, shall pass to the said United States, under the stipulations therein expressed.

And the said Colonel Commandant, Don Jose Callava, has, in consequence, at this present time, made to the Commissioner of the United States, Major General Andrew Jackson, in this public cession, a delivery of keys of the town of Pensacola, of the archives, documents and other articles in the inventory before mentioned, declaring that he releases from their oath of allegiance to Spain, the citizens and inhabitants of West Florida, who may choose to remain under the dominion of the United States.

And that this important and solemn act may be in perpetual memory, the within named have signed the same in English and Spanish languages, and have sealed with their respective seals, and caused to be attested by their Secretaries of Commission, the day and year aforesaid.

(Signed)   ANDREW JACKSON
Commissioner on the part of the U.S.
(Signed)   JOSE CALLAVA,
Commissioner on the part of the H.C.M.

By order of the Commissioners on the part of the United States.
R.K. CALL,
Secretary of the Commission.

PROCLAMATION OF

MAJOR GENERAL ANDREW JACKSON

By Major General Andrew Jackson, Governor of the Provinces
of the Floridas, exercising the powers of the Captain General and of the Intendant of the Island of Cuba, over the said Provinces, and of the Governors of said Provinces respectively.

WHEREAS, by the treaty concluded between the United States and Spain, on the 22d day of February, 1819, and duly ratified, the Provinces of the Floridas were ceded by Spain to the United States, and the possession of the said Provinces is now in the United States:

And whereas, the Congress of the United States, on the third day of March, in the present year, did enact, that until the end of the first Session of the seventeenth Congress, unless provision for the temporary government of said provinces be sooner made by Congress, all the military, civil and judicial powers exercised by the officers of the existing government of the said provinces, shall be vested in such person or persons, and shall be exercised in such manner as the President of the United States shall direct, for the maintaining the inhabitants of said territories in the free enjoyment of their Liberty, Property, and Religion; and the President of the United States, has, by his commission bearing date the tenth day of said March, invested me with all the powers and charged me with the several duties heretofore held and exercised by the Captain General, Intendant and Governors aforesaid:

I have therefore thought fit to issue this my Proclamation, making known the premises, and to declare that the government heretofore exercised over the said Provinces under the authority of Spain, has ceased, and that of the United States of America is established over the same; that the inhabitants thereof will be incorporated in the union of the United States, as soon as may be consistent with the principles of the Federal Constitution, and admitted to the enjoyment of all the privileges, rights, and immunities of the citizens of the United States—that in the mean time, they shall be maintained and protected in the free enjoyment of their liberty, property, and the religion they profess; that all laws and municipal regulations which were in existence at the cessation of the late government, remain in full force, and all civil officers, charged with their execution, except those whose powers have been specially vested in me, and except also, such officers as have been intrusted with the collection of the revenue, are continued in their functions, furing the pleasure of the Governor for the time being, or until provision shall otherwise be made.

And I do hereby exhort and enjoin all the inhabitants and other persons within the said Provinces, to be faithful and true in their allegiance to the United States, and obedient to the authorities of the same, under full assurance that their just rights will be under the guardianship of the United States, and will be maintained from all force and violence from without or within.

Given at Pensacola, this 17th day of July, one thousand eight hundred and twenty-one.

ANDREW JACKSON

By the Governor,
R.K. CALL,
  Acting Secretary, West Florida.

ORDINANCES OF

MAJOR GENERAL ANDREW JACKSON

By Major General Andrew Jackson, Governor of the Provinces
  of the Floridas, exercising the powers of the Captain General and of the Intendant of the Island of Cuba, and of the Governors of said Provinces respectively:

ORDAIN:

Sec. 1. That the said Provinces be divided as follows:

All the country lying between the Perdido and Suwaney rivers, with all the islands therein, shall form one country to be called Escambia.

All the country lying East of the river Suwaney, and every part of the ceded territories, not designated as belonging to the former country, shall form a country to be called St. Johns.

Sec. 2. In each of said countries, and for the government thereof, there shall be established a court, to be designated a county court, and to be composed of five justices of the peace, any three of whom shall form a quorum, and the eldest by appointment to be president of said court, whose jurisdiction shall extend to all civil cases originating in the country, where the matter in controversy shall exceed twenty dollars, and to all criminal cases savings to the parties the right of appeal to the Governor, in all cases above the sum of five hundred dollars; and that there shall be no execution for a capital offense, until the warrant of the Governor be first had and obtained.

Sec. 3. That the judicial proceedings in all civil cases shall be conducted, except as to the examination of witnesses, according to the course of the existing laws, or to the laws of Spain, and in criminal cases, according to the course of the common law: that is, no person shall be held to answer for a capital, or otherwise infamous crime, unless on a presentment or indictment of a Grand Jury, and in all criminal cases, the accused shall enjoy the right to a speedy, and public trial, by an impartial Jury of the county wherein the crime shall have been committed; and to be informed of the nature and cause of the accusation, to be confronted with the witnesses against him, and to have compulsory process for obtaining witnesses in his favor and to have the assistance of counsel for his defence.

Sec. 4. There shall be a clerk appointed for each of said county courts, who shall receive for his services, such compensation as the court for which he is appointed may from time to time, and in each suit, tax or allow; and there shall also be a sheriff appointed to ech court, to execute the process thereof, whose services shall be compensated by the court to which he is appointed in like manner as is provided for the clerk—and the said clerk and sheriff shall give bond to the presiding justice, for the faithful discharge of their duties.

Sec. 5. Each County Court shall hold

quarterly sessions, and to continue the same until all the business pending therein shall be disposed of. The first session to be held at Pensacola, on the first Monday of August next, for the county of Escambia—and, at St. Augustine, on the second Monday of September next, for the county of St. Johns—with the power to adjourn the same from time to time.

Sec. 6. There shall not be less than ten Justices of the Peace commissioned for each country, whose jurisdiction shall extend to all civil cases, not exceeding fifty dollars; saving to the parties or suitors, an appeal to the county court, in all cases wherein the matter in dispute shall exceed the sum of twenty dollars—and shall also be authorized in all criminal cases to exact surety for good behavior, and to take recognizances in cases bailable, for the appearance of the accused before the county courts.

Sec. 7. That the examination of all witnesses within the jurisdiction of the courts, except when their personal attendance cannot be procured, shall be conducted viva voce and in open court: that the parties may conduct their suits in person, or by such counsel as they may choose: Provided, that the said counsel or counsellors, shall have been duly licensed to practice in the courts of said ceded territories by the Governor.

Sec. 8. The Alcaldes shall continue to exercise the powers of Judges of probate, Registers of Wills, Notaries Public, of Justices of the Peace, and such other powers, appertaining to the said offices, as have not been otherwise distributed, saving the right of appeal to the county court in all cases.

Sec. 9. That the judges of the said county courts shall have power to impose such taxes upon the inhabitants of their counties respectively, as in their discretion may be necessary to meet and defray the expenses which may be incurred in carrying this ordinance into effect.

Sec. 10. That the said county courts shall have and exercise the powers of directing by special venire or otherwise, the summoning of all Jurors, Grand as well as petit.

Sec. 11. That the said courts shall have the power of creating and regulating their process and proceedings from time to time, as they may deem necessary, and shall as soon as convenient after their organization, prepare and report a fee bill to the Governor for his approbation.

Sec. 12. That the said court shall have, and exercise beyond the limits of Pensacola and St. Augustine, the power of granting and recalling licenses or commissions for inkeepers, retailers of liquors of every description and keepers for billiard tables, and to require of them such surety as they may deem proper, and impose such price for such license as in their opinion may be reasonable.

Sec. 13. That it shall be the duty of said courts in regulating their process and proceedings to confine the parties strictly to the merits of their cause, and to cause all useless matter, as well as unnecessary form to be expunged from the pleadings at the expense of the party introducing the same, so that justice may be administered, in the most simple, cheap, and speedy manner.

Sec. 14. In all criminal cases, the process and indictment shall be in the name of the United States, and there shall be appointed a prosecuting Attorney for each of the said counties, who shall receive in each case, a reasonable compensation, to be taxed by the court.

Sec. 15. That the police of the roads and bridges without the limits of Pensacola and St. Augustine, shall be under the immediate direction of the said county courts; the police of the city to be exclusively confided to the Mayor and Aldermen.

Pensacola, July 21st, 1821.

(Signed)   ANDREW JACKSON

By the Governor:
    R.K. CALL,
        Acting Secretary of West Florida.

AN ORDINANCE

Prescribing the mode of carrying into effect the 6th
        article of the Treaty of Amity; settlement of differences and limits between the United States of America and his Catholic Majesty.

Whereas by the sixth article of the said treaty, it is among other things provided;

that on the entrance of the ceded territories into the Union, the inhabitants thereof shall be 'admitted to the enjoyment of all the privileges, rights and immunities of the citizens of the United States.' Now, therefore, as well with a view to guard against impositions, that may be practiced by foreigners, as to secure to the inhabitants their free choice to become citizens of the United States, under the provisions of the said treaty.

Sec. 1. I do ordain, That the Mayor of the City of Pensacola, and such other persons as may be appointed for the purpose in any town or county of these provinces, shall open a register, and cause to be inscribed the name, age, and occupation of every free male inhabitant of such town or county, who may be desirous to profit by the provisions of the sixth article of the treaty, so as aforesaid in part recited, provided the person or inhabitant who may thus desire to have his name inscribed, shall first satisfy the mayor or such other persons as may be appointed to open Registers; that he was really an inhabitant of the ceded territory on the 17th day of July 1821: and provided also, that he will of his own free will and accord, abjure all foreign allegiance, and take the oath of allegiance prescribed by the laws of the United States.

Sec. 2. That the office or register shall continue open for and during the space of twelve months, when the same shall be closed, and a copy thereof transmitted under the seal of the said Mayor, or other persons appointed to open registers to the secretaries of the said territories.

Sec. 3. That from and after the period that the said register shall be so closed, no other free male inhabitant above the age of twenty one, and entitled, to make his election as aforesaid, shall be, within the ceded territories, entitled to any of the rights, privileges and immunities of a citizen of the United States, but shall to all intents and purposes be considered as foreigners, and subject to the laws of the United States, in relation to aliens.

Sec. 4. It shall be the duty of heads of families within the said provinces, being desirous to profit by this act, to furnish the Mayor or such other persons as may be appointed to open registers, with the name and age of every free male member of his family, and the said Mayor shall cause the same to be inscribed on the register, as before provided for.

Sec. 5. In order to guard the more effectually against impositions, as well as to give to the inhabitants the security which citizenship will afford them abroad. It is further ordained, That the Secretary or Secretaries of the ceded territories, grant to such inhabitants as may be desirous of receiving the same, certificates of citizenship, he or they being first satisfied that the provisions of this ordinance shall have been complied with.

Sec. 6. The evidence upon which the Secretary or Secretaries shall proceed to grant certificates of citizenship shall be a certificate of the clerk of the Mayor, or such other persons as may be appointed to open registers, that the applicant has complied with the requisitions of this ordinance, upon the receipt of which it shall be the duty of the Secretary or Secretaries, to grant to all and every such applicant or applicants, certificates of citizenship, for which the said clerk and Secretary shall be entitled to one dollar each, and for every name entered on the register the Mayor or other person authorized to open the same shall be entitled to one dollar.

Pensacola, 21st July, 1821

(Signed)   ANDREW JACKSON

By the Governor:
R.K. CALL,
Acting Secretary of West Florida.

CHEROKEE NATION v. GEORGIA
1831

Suit for injunction to restrain the State of Georgia. In 1827 the Cherokee Indians, occupying extensive lands in northwestern Georgia, set up a government and declared themselves an independent nation. Thereupon the legislature of Georgia passed resolutions alleging ownership of all Cherokee territory and extending the laws of Georgia over the Cherokee Indians, and annulling all laws, usages and customs of the Indians. The Indians appealed to the

Supreme Court for an injunction to prevent the execution of these laws. The opinion of Marshall is notable for its definition of the legal relations of the Indians with the United States government: the Indians constitute not foreign nations but domestic dependent nations in a state of pupilage. See, Beveridge, Marshall, Vol. IV, p. 539 ff.; A. Abel, 'History of Events Resulting in Indian Consolidation West of the Mississippi River,' in Am. Hist. Assoc. Reports, 1906, Vol. I; and references in Docs. No. 141-142.

Marshall, C.J. This bill is brought by the Cherokee nation, praying an injunction to restrain the state of Georgia from the execution of certain laws of that state, which, as is alleged, go directly to annihilate the Cherokee as a political society, and to seize for the use of Georgia, the lands of the nation which have been assured to them by the United States, in solemn treaties repeatedly made and still in force.

If courts were permitted to indulge their sympathies, a case better calculated to excite them can scarcely be imagined. A people, once numerous, powerful, and truly independent, found by our ancestors in the quiet and uncontrolled possession of an ample domain, gradually sinking beneath our superior policy, our arts and our arms, have yielded their lands, by successive treaties, each of which contains a solemn guarantee of the residue, until they retain no more of their formerly extensive territory than is deemed necessary to their comfortable subsistence. To preserve this remnant, the present application is made.

Before we can look into the merits of the case, a preliminary inquiry presents itself. Has this court jurisdiction of the cause? The third article of the constitution describes the extent of the judicial power. The second closes an enumeration of the cases to which it is extended, with 'controversies between a state or citizens thereof, and foreign states, citizens or subjects.' A subsequent clause of the same section gives the supreme court original jurisdiction, in all cases in which a state shall be a party. The party defendant may then unquestionably be sued in this court. May the plaintiff sue in it? Is the Cherokee nation a foreign state, in the sense in which that term is used in the constitution? The counsel for the plaintiffs have maintained the affirmative of this proposition with great earnestness and ability. So much of the argument as was intended to prove the character of the Cherokees as a state, as a distinct political society, separated from others, capable of managing its own affairs and governing itself, has in the opinion of a majority of the judges, been completely successful. They have been uniformly treated as a state, from the settlement of our country. The numerous treaties made with them by the United States, recognize them as a people capable of maintaining the relations of peace and war, of being responsible in their political character for any violation of their engagements, or for any aggression committed on the citizens of the United States, by any individual of their community. Laws have been enacted in the spirit of these treaties. The acts of our government plainly recognise the Cherokee nation as a state, and the courts are bound by those acts.

A question of much more difficulty remains. Do the Cherokee constitute a foreign state in the sense of the constitution? The counsel have shown conclusively, that they are not a state of the Union, and have insisted that, individually, they are aliens, not owing allegiance to the United States. An aggregate of aliens composing a state must, they say, be a foreign state; each individual being foreign, the whole must be foreign.

This argument is imposing, but we must examine it more closely, before we yield to it. The condition of the Indians in relation to the United States is, perhaps, unlike that of any other nations not owing a common allegiance, are foreign to each other. The term foreign nation is, with strict propriety, applicable by either to the other. But the relation of the Indians to the United States is marked by peculiar and cardinal distinctions which exist nowhere else. The Indian territory is admitted to compose a part of the United States. In all our maps, geographical treaties, histories and laws, it is so considered. In all our intercourse with foreign nations, in our commercial regulations, in any attempt at intercourse between and foreign nations, they are considered as within the jurisdictional limits of the United States subject to many of those restraints which are imposed upon our own citizens. They acknowledge themselves, in their treaties, to be under the protection of the United States, they admit, that the United States shall have the sole and exclusive right of regulating the trade with them, and managing all their affairs as they think proper; and the Cherokees in particular were allowed by the treaty of Hopewell, which preceded the constitution 'to send a deputy of their choice, whenever they think fit, to congress.' Treaties were made with some tribes, by the state of New York, under a then unsettled construction of the confederation, by which they ceded all their lands to that state, taking back a limited grant to themselves, in which they admit their dependence. Though the Indians are acknowledged to have an unquestionable, and heretofore unquestioned, right to the lands they occupy, until that right shall be extinguished by a voluntary cession to our government; yet it may well be doubted, whether those tribes which reside within the acknowledged boundaries of the United States can with accuracy, be denominated foreign nations. They may, more correctly, perhaps be denominated domestic dependent nations. They occupy a territory to which we assert a title independent of their will, which must take effect in point of possession, when their right of possession ceases. Meanwhile, they are in a state of pupilage; their relation to the United States resembles that of a ward to his guardian. They look to our government for protection; rely upon its kindness and its power; appeal to it for relief to their wants, and address the president as their great father. They and their country are considered by foreign nations, as well as by ourselves, as being so completely under the sovereignty and dominion of the United States, that any attempt to acquire their lands, or to form a political connection with them would be considered by all as an invasion of our territory and an act of hostility. These considerations go far to support the opinion, that the framers of our constitution had not the Indian tribes in view, when they opened the courts of the Union to controversies between a state or the citizens thereof and foreign states.

In considering this subject, the habits and usages of the Indians, in their intercourse with their white neighbors, ought not to be entirely disregarded. At the time the constitution was framed, the idea of appealing to an American court of justice for an assertion of right or a redress of wrong, had perhaps never entered the mind of an Indian or of his tribe. Their appeal was to the tomahawk, or to the government. This was well understood by the statesmen who framed the constitution of the United States, and might furnish some reason for omitting to enumerate them among the parties who might sue in the courts of the Union. Be this as it may, the peculiar relations between the United States and the Indians occupying our territories are such, that we should feel much difficulty in considering them as designated by the term foreign state, were there no other part of the constitution which might shed light on the meaning of these words. But we think that in construing them, considerable aid is furnished by that clause in the eighth section of the third article, which empowers congress to 'regulate commerce with foreign nations, and among the several states, and with the Indian tribes.' In this clause, they are clearly as contradistinguished, by a name appropriate to themselves, from foreign nations, and among the several states composing the Union. They are designated by a distinct appellation; and as this appellation can be applied to neither of the others, neither can the application distinguishing either of the others be, in fair construction, applied to them. The objects to which the power of regulating commerce might be directed, are divided into three distinct classes-foreign nations, the several states, the Indian tribes. When forming this article, the convention considered them as entirely distinct. We cannot assure that the distinction was lost, in framing a subsequent article, unless there be something in its language to authorize the assumption.

The counsel for the plaintiffs contend, that the words 'Indian tribes' were introduced into the article, empowering congress to regulate commerce, for the purpose of removing those doubts in which the management of Indian affairs was involved by the language of the ninth article of the confederation. Intending to give the whole of managing those affairs to the government about to be instituted, the convention conferred it explicitly; and omitted those qualifications which embarrassed the exercise of it, as granted in the confederation. This may be admitted, without weakening the construction which has been intimated. Had the Indian tribes been foreign nations, in the view of the convention, this exclusive power of regulating intercourse with them might have been, and, most probably, would have been, specifically given, in language indicating that idea, not in language contradistinguishing them from foreign nations. Congress might have been empowered 'to regulate commerce with foreign nations, including the Indian tribes, and among the several states.' This language would have suggested itself to statesmen who considered the Indian tribes as foreign nations, and were yet desirous of mentioning them particularly.

It has been also said, that the same words have not necessarily the same meaning attached to them, when found in different parts of the same instrument; their meaning is controlled by the context. This is undoubltedly true. In common language, the same word has various meanings, and the peculiar sense in which it is used in any sentence, is to be determined by the context. This may not be equally true with respect to proper names. 'Foreign nations' is a general term, the application of which to Indian tribes, when used in the American constitution, is, at best, extremely questionable. In one article, in which a power is given to be exercised in regard to foreign nations generally, and to the Indian tribes particularly, they are mentioned as separate, in terms clearly contradistinguishing them from each other. We perceive plainly, that the constitution, in this article, does not comprehend Indian tribes in the general term 'foreign nation;' not, we presume, because a tribe may not be a nation, but because it is not foreign to the United States. When, afterwards, the term 'foreign state' is introduced, we cannot impute to the convention, the intention to desert its former meaning, and to comprehend Indian tribes within it, unless the context force that construction on us. We find nothing in the context, and nothing in the subject of that article, which leads to it.

The court has bestowed its best attention on this question, and, after mature deliberation, the majority is of opinion, that an Indian tribe or nation within the United States is not a foreign state, in the sense of the constitution, and cannot maintain an action in the courts of the United States.

A serious additional objection exists to the jurisdiction of the court. Is the matter of the bill the proper subject for judicial inquiry and decision? It seeks to restrain a state from the forcible exercise of legislative power over a neighboring people, asserting their independence; their right to which the state denies. On several of the matters alleged in the bill, for example, on the laws making it criminal to exercise the usual powers of self-government in their own country, by the Cherokee nation, this court cannot interpose; at least, in the form in which those matters are presented.

That part of the bill which respects the land occupied by the Indians, and prays the aid of the court to protect their possession, may be doubtful. The mere question of right might, perhaps, be decided by this court, in a proper case, with proper parties. But the court is asked to do more than decide on the title. The bill requires us to control the legislature of Georgia, and to restrain the exertion of its physical force. The propriety of such an interposition by the court may be well questionable; it savors too much of the exercise of political power, to be within the proper province of the judicial department. But the opinion on the point respecting parties makes it unnecessary to decide this question.

If it be true, that the Cherokee nation have rights, this is not the tribunal in which those rights are to be asserted. If it be true, that wrongs have been inflicted, and that still greater are to be apprehended, this is not the tribunal which can redress the past or prevent the future. The motion for injunction is denied. STORY, J. and THOMPSON, J. dissenting.

TREATY WITH THE FLORIDA TRIBES OF INDIANS
September 18, 1823

Article I. The undersigned chiefs and warriors, for themselves and their tribes, have appealed to the humanity, and thrown themselves on, and have promised to continue under, the protection of the United States, and of no other nation, power, or sovereign; and, in consideration of the promises and stipulations hereinafter made, do cede and relinquish all claim or title which they may have to the whole Territory of Florida, with the exception of such district of country as shall herein be allotted to them.

Article II. The Florida tribes of Indians will hereafter be concentrated and confined to the following metes and boundaries: commencing five miles north of Okehumke, running in a direct line to a point five miles west of Setarky's settlement, on the waters of Amazura, (or Withlahuchie river,) leaving said settlement two miles south of the line; from thence, in a direct line, to the south end of the Big Hammock, to include Chickuchate; continuing, in the same direction, for five miles beyond the said Hammock—provided said point does not approach nearer than fifteen miles the sea coast of the Gulf of Mexico; if it does, the said line will terminate at that distance from the sea coast; thence, south, twelve miles; thence in a south 30° east direction, until the same shall strike within five miles of the main branch of Charlotte river; thence, in a due east direction, to within twenty miles of the Atlantic coast; thence, north, fifteen west, for fifty miles and from this last, to the beginning point.

Article III. The United States will take the Florida Indians under the care and patronage, and will afford them protection against all persons whatsoever; provided they conform to the laws of the United States, and refrain from making war, or giving any insult to any foreign nation, without having first obtained the permission and consent of the United States: And, in consideration of the appeal and cession made in the first article of this treaty, by the aforesaid chiefs and warriors,

the United States promise to distribute among the tribes, as soon as concentrated, under the direction of their agent, implements of husbandry, and stock of cattle and hogs, to the amount of six thousand dollars, and an annual sum of five thousand dollars a year, for twenty successive years, to be distributed as the President of the United States shall direct, through the Secretary of War, or his Superintendents and Agent of Indian Affairs.

Article IV. The United States promise to quaranty to the said tribes the peaceable possession of the district of country herein assigned them, reserving the right of opening through it such roads, as may, from time to time, be deemed necessary; and to restrain and prevent all white persons from hunting, settling, or otherwise intruding upon it. But any citizen of the United States, being lawful authorized for that purpose, shall be permitted to pass and repass through the said district, and to navigate the waters thereof, without any hindrance, toll, or exaction, from said tribes.

Article V. For the purpose of facilitating the removal of the said tribes to the district of country allotted them, and, as a compensation for the losses sustained, or the inconveniences to which they may be exposed by said removal, the United States will furnish them with rations of corn, meat, and salt, for twelve months, commencing on the first day of February next; and they further agree to compensate those individuals who have been compelled to abandon improvements on lands, not embraced within the limits allotted, to the amount of four thousand five hundred dollars, to be distributed among the sufferers, in a ratio to each, proportional to the value of the improvements abandoned. The United States, further agree to furnish a sum, not exceeding two thousand dollars, to be expended by their agent, to facilitate the transportation of the different tribes to the point of concentration designated.

Article VI. An agent, sub-agent, and interpreter, shall be appointed, to reside within the Indian boundary aforesaid, to watch over the interests of said tribes; and the United States further stipulate, as an evidence of their humane policy towards said tribes, who have appealed to their liberality, to allow for the establishment of a school at the agency, one thousand dollars per year for twenty successive years; and one thousand dollars per year, for the same period, for the support of a gun and blacksmith, with the expenses incidental to his shop.

Article VII. The chiefs and warriors, aforesaid, for themselves and tribes, stipulate to be active and vigilant in the preventing the retreating to, or passing through, of the district of country assigned them, of any absconding slaves, or fugitives from justice; and further agree, to use all necessary exertions to apprehend and deliver the same to the agent, who shall receive orders to compensate them agreeably to the trouble and expenses incurred.

Article VIII. A commissioner, or commissioners, with a surveyor, shall be appointed, by the President of the United States, to run, and mark, (blazing fore and aft the trees) the line as devined in the second article of this treaty, who shall be attended by a chief or warrior, to be designated by a council of their own tribes, and who shall receive, while so employed, a daily compensation of three dollars.

Article IX. The undersigned chiefs and warriors, for themselves and tribes, having objected to their concentration within the limits described in the second article of this treaty, under the impression that the said limits did not contain a sufficient quantity of good land to subsist them, and for no other reason: it is, therefore, expressly understood, between the United States and the aforesaid chiefs and warriors, that, should the country embraced in the said limits, upon examination by the Indian agent and the commissioner, or commissioners, to be appointed under the 8th article of this treaty, be by them considered insufficient for the support of the said Indian tribes; then the north line, as defined in the 2d article of this treaty, shall be removed so far north as to embrace a sufficient quantity of good tillable land.

Article X. The undersigned chiefs and warriors, for themselves and tribes, have expressed to the commissioners their unlimited confidence in their agent, Col. Gad Humphreys, and their interpreter, Stephen Richards, and, as an evidence of their gratitude for their services and humane treatment, and brotherly attentions to their wants, request that one mile square, embracing the improvements of Enehe Mathla, at Tallahassee (said improvements to be considered as the centre) be conveyed, in fee simple, as a present to Col. Gad Humphreys.—And they further request, that one mile square, at the Ochesse Bluffs, embracing Stephen Richard's field on the said Bluffs, be conveyed in fee simple, as a present to said Stephen Richards. The commissioners accord in sentiment with the undersigned chiefs and warriors, and recommend a compliance with their wishes to the President and Senate of the United States; but the disapproval, on the part of the said authorities, of this article, shall, in no wise, affect the other articles and stipulations concluded on in this treaty.

In testimony whereof, the Commissioners, William P. Duval,

James Gadsen, and Bernard Segui, and the undersigned Chiefs and Warriors have hereunto subscribed their names and affixed their seals. Done at Camp, on Moultrie Creek, in the Territory of Florida, this eighteenth day of September, one thousand eight hundred and twenty-three, and of the Independence of the United States the forty-eighth.

WILLIAM P. DUVALL,
JAMES GADSEN,
BERNARD SEGUI.

Nea Mathla,	Holatefixico,
Tokose Mathia,	Chefixico Hajo,
Ninnee Homata	Lathloa Mathla,
Tustenuky,	Senufky,
Miconope,	Alak Hajo,
Nocosee Ahola,	Fabelustee Hajo,
John Blunt,	Octahamico
Otlemata,	Tusteneck Hajo
Tuskeeneha,	Okoskee Amathla,
Tuski Hajo,	Ocheeney Tustenuky,
Econchatimico,	Phillip,
Emoteley,	Charley Amathla,
Mulatto King,	John Hoponey,
Chocholohano,	Rat Head,
Ematlochee,	Holatta Amathla,
Wokse Holata,	Fosshatchimico.
Amathla Hajo,	

Signed, sealed, and delivered, in presence of George Murray, Secretary to the Commission. G. Humphreys, Indian Agent, Stephen Richards, Interpreter. Isaac N. Cox. J. Erving, Capt. 4th Artillery, Harvey Brown, Lieut. 4th Artillery. C. D'Espinville, Lieut. 4th Artillery. Jno. B. Scott, Lieut. 4th Artillery. William Travers. Horatio S. Dexter.

******

ADDITIONAL ARTICLE
September 8, 1823

Whereas Neo Mathla, John Blunt, Tuski Hajo, Mulatto King, Emathlochee, and Econchatimico, six of the principal Chiefs of the Florida Indians, and parties to the treaty to which this article has been annexed, have warmly appealed to the Commissioners for permission to remain in the district of country now inhabited by them; and, in consideration of their friendly disposition, and past services to the United States, it is, therefore, stipulated, between the United States and the aforesaid Chiefs, that the following reservations shall be surveyed, and marked by the Commissioner, or Commissioners, to be appointed under the 8th article of this Treaty: For the use of Nea Mathla and his connections, two miles square, embracing the Tuphulga village, on the waters of Rocky Comfort Creek. For Blunt and Tuski Hajo, a reservation, commencing on the Apalachicola, one mile below Tuski Hajo's improvements, running up said river four miles due west of the beginning; thence, east, to the beginning point. For Mulatto King and Emathlochee, a reservation, commencing on the Apalachicola, at a point to include Yellow Hair's improvements; thence, up said river, for four miles; thence, west, one mile; thence, southerly, to a point one mile west of the beginning; and thence, east, to the beginning point. For Econchatimico, a reservation, commencing on the Chatahoochie, one mile below Econcha-timico's house; thence, up said river, for four miles; thence, one mile, west; thence, southerly, to a point one mile west of the beginning; thence, east, to the beginning point. The United States promise to guaranty the peaceable possession of the said reservations, as defined, to the aforesaid chiefs and their descendents only, so long as they shall continue to occupy, improve, or cultivate, the same; but in the event of the abandonment of all, or either of the reservations, by the chief or chiefs, to whom they have been allotted, the reservation, or reservations, so abandoned, shall revert to the United States, as included in the cession made in the first article of this treaty. It is further understood, that the names of the individuals remaining on the reservations aforesaid, shall be furnished, by the chiefs in whose favour the reservations have been made, to the Superintendent or agent of Indian Affairs, in the Territory of Florida; and that no other individuals shall be received or permitted to remain within said reservations, without the previous consent of the Superintendent or agent aforesaid; And, as the aforesaid Chiefs are authorized to select the individuals remaining with them, so they shall each be separately held responsible for the peaceable conduct of their towns, or the individuals residing on the reservations allotted them. It is further understood, between the parties, that this agreement is not intended to prohibit the voluntary removal, at any future period, of all or either of the aforesaid Chiefs and their connections, to the district of country south, allotted to the Florida Indians, by the second article of this Treaty, whenever either, or all may think proper to make such an election; the United States reserving the right of ordering, for any outrage or misconduct, the aforesaid Chiefs, or either of them, with their connections, within the district of country south, aforesaid. It is further stipulated, by the United States, that, of the six thousand dollars, appropriated for implements of husbandry, stock, &c. in the third article of this Treaty, eight hundred dollars shall be distributed, in the same manner, among the aforesaid chiefs and their towns; and it is understood, that, of the annual sum of five thousand dollars, to be distributed by the President of the United States, they will receive their proportion. It is further stipulated, that, of the four thousand five hundred dollars, and two thousand dollars, provided for by the 5th article of this Treaty, for the payment of improvements and transportation, five hundred dollars shall be awarded to Neo Mathla, as a compensation for the improvements abandoned by him, as well as to meet the expenses he will be unavoidably be exposed to, by his own removal, and that of his connections.

In testimony whereof, the Commissioners, William P. Duval,

James Gadsden, and Bernard Segui, and the undersigned Chiefs and Warriors, have hereunto subscribed their names, and affixed their seals. Done at Camp, on Moultrie Creek, in the Territory of Florida, this eighteenth day of September, one thousand eight hundred and twenty-three, and of the independence of the United States the forty-eighth.

WM. P. DUVAL,
JAMES GADSDEN,
BERNARD SEGUI,

Nea Mathla,	Mulatto King,
John Blunt	Emathlochee,
Tuski Hajo,	Econchatimico.

Signed, sealed, and delivered, in presence of George Murray, Secretary to the Commission. Ja. W. Ripley. G. Humphreys, Indian Agent. Stephen Richards, Interpreter.

The following statement shows the number of men retained by the Chiefs, who have reservations made them, at their respective villages:

	Number of Men
Blount,	43
Cochran,	45
Mulatto King,	30
Emathlochee	28
Econchatimico	38
Neo Mathla	30
Total	214

To the Indian names are subjoined a mark and seal.

******

TREATY WITH THE SEMINOLES
May 9, 1832

The Seminole Indians, regarding with just respect, the solicitude manifested by the President of the United States for the improvement of their condition, by recommending a removal to a country more suitable to their habits and wants more than the one they at present occupy in the Territory of Florida, are willing that their confidential chiefs, Jumper, Fuck-a-lus-ti-had-jo, Charley Emarthla, Coi-had-jo, Holati-Emartla, Ya-ha-hadjo, Sam Jones, accompanied by their agent Major Phagan, and their faithful interpreter Abraham, should be sent at the expense of the United States as early as convenient to examine the country assigned to the Creeks west of the Mississippi river, and should they be satisfied with the character of that country, and of the favorable disposition of the Creeks to reunite with the Seminoles as one people; the articles of the compact and agreement, herein stipulated at Payne's landing on the Ocklewaha river, this ninth day of May, one thousand eight hundred and thirty-two, between James Gadsden, for and in behalf of the Government of the United States, and the undersigned chiefs and head-men for and in behalf of the Seminole Indians, shall be binding on the respective parties.

ARTICLE I. The Seminole Indians relinquish to the United States, all claims to the lands they at present occupy in the Territory of Florida, and agree to emigrate to the country assigned to the Creeks, west of the Mississippi river; it being understood that an additional extent of territory, proportioned to their numbers, will be added to the Creek country, and that the Seminoles will be received as a constituent part of the Creek nation, and be re-admitted to all the priviledges as members of the same.

ARTICLE II. For and in consideration of the relinquishment of claim in the first article of this agreement, and in full compensation for all the improvements, which may have been made on the lands, thereby ceded; the United States stipulate to pay to the Seminole Indians, fifteen thousand, four hundred (15,400) dollars, to be divided among the chiefs and warriors of the several towns, in a ratio proportioned to their population, the respective proportions of each to be paid on their arrival in the country they consent to remove it; it being understood that their faithful interpreters Abraham and Cudjo shall shall receive two hundred dollars each of the above sum, in full remuneration for the improvements to be abandoned on the lands now cultivated by them.

ARTICLE III. The United States agree to distribute as they arrive at their new homes in the Creek Territory, west of the Mississippi river, a blanket and a homespun frock, to each of the warriors, women and children of the Seminole tribe of Indians.

ARTICLE IV. The United States agree to extend the annuity for the support of the blacksmith, provided for in the sixth article of the treaty at Camp Moultrie for ten (10) years beyond the period therein stipulated, and in addition to the other annuities secured under that treaty; the United States agree to pay the sum of three thousand (3,000) dollars a year for fifteen (15) years, commencing after the removal of the whole tribe; these sums to be added to the Creek annuities, and the whole amount to be so divided, that the chiefs and warriors of the Seminole Indians may receive their equitable proportion of the same as members of the Creek confederation—

ARTICLE V. The United States will take the cattle belonging to the Seminoles at the valuation of some discreet person to be appointed by the President, and the same shall be paid for in money to the respective owners, after their arrival at their new homes; or other cattle such as may be desired will be furnished them, notice being given through their agent of their wishes upon this subject, before their removal, that time may be afforded to supply the demand.

ARTICLE VI. The Seminoles being anxious to be relieved from repeated vexatious demands for slaves and other property, alleged to have been stolen and destroyed by them, so that they may remove unembarrassed to their new homes; the United States stipulate to have the same property investigated, and to liquidate such as may be satisfactorily established, provided the amount does not exceed seven thousand (7,000) dollars.—

ARTICLE VII. The Seminole Indians will remove within three (3) years after the ratification of this agreement, and the expenses of their removal shall be defrayed by the United States, and such subsistence shall also be furnished them for a term not exceeding twelve (12) months, after their arrival at their new residence; as in the opinion of the President, their numbers and circumstances may require, the emigration to commence as early as practicable in the year eighteen hundred and thirty-three (1833,) and with those Indians at present occupying the Big swamp, and other parts of the country beyond the limits as defined in the second article of the treaty concluded at Camp Moultrie creek, so that the whole of that proportion of the Seminoles may be removed within the year aforesaid, and the remainder of the tribe, in about equal proportions, during the subsequent years of eighteen hundred and thirty-four and five, (1834 and 1835.)—

In testimony whereof, the commissioner James Gadsden and the undersigned chiefs and Head-men of the Seminole Indians, have hereunto subscribed their names and affixed their seals—Done at Camp at Payne's landing on the Ocklewaha river in the Territory of Florida on this ninth day of May, one thousand eight hundred and thirty-two, and of the Independence of the United States of America the fifty-sixth.

JAMES GADSDEN, (L.S)

Holati Emartla,	Tokose-Emartla,
Jumper,	or Jno. Hicks,
Fuck-ta-lus-ta	Cat-sha-Tusta
Hadjo,	nuck-i,
Charley Emartla,	Hola-at-a-Meco,
Coa Hadjo,	Hitch-it-i-Meco,
Ar-pi-uck-i, or	E-ne-hah,
Sam Jones,	Ya-ha-emartla
Ha-ha Hadjo,	Chup-ko,
Meco-Noha,	Moke-his-she-lar-ni.

WITNESSES:—Douglas Vass, Secretary to Commission. John Phagan, Agent. Stephen Richards, Inpt. Abraham, Interpreter, Cudjo, Interpreter. Erastus Rogers. B. Joscan.

To the Indian names are subjoined marks.

TREATY WITH THE APPALACHICOLA BAND
October 11, 1832

The undersigned chiefs, for and in behalf of themselves and warriors, surrender to the United States, all their right, title and interest to a reservation of land made for their benefit, in the additional article of the treaty, concluded at Camp Moultrie, in the Territory of Florida, on the 18th of September, eighteen hundred and twenty-three, and which is described in said article, 'as commencing on the Appalachicola, one mile below Tuski Hajo's improvements, running up said river four miles, thence west two miles, thence southerly to a point due west of the beginning, thence east to the beginning point,' and agree to remove with their warriors and families, now occupying said reservation, and amounting in all to (256) two hundred and fifty-six souls, to the west of the Mississippi river, beyond the limits of the States and Territories of the United States of America.

ARTICLE II. For, and in consideration of said surrender, and to meet the charges of a party to explore immediately the country west in search of a home more suitable to their habits, than the one at present occupied, and in full compensation for all the expenses of emigration, and subsistence for themselves and party: The United States agree to pay to the undersigned chiefs and their warriors, thirteen thousand dollars; three thousand dollars in cash, the receipt of which is herewith acknowledged, and ten thousand dollars whenever they have completed their arrangements, and have commenced the removal of their whole party.

ARTICLE III. The undersigned chiefs, with their warriors and families, will evacuate the reservation of land surrendered by the first article of this agreement, on or before the first of November, eighteen hundred and thirty-three; but should unavoidable circumstances prevent the conclusion of the necessary preparatory arrangements by that time, it is expected that the indulgence of the government of the United States will be reasonably extended for a term, not to exceed however another year.

ARTICLE IV. The United States further stipulate to continue to Blunt and Davy (formerly Tuski Hajo deceased) the Chiefs of the towns now consenting to emigrate, their proportion of the annuity of five thousand dollars which they at present draw, and to which they are entitled under the treaty of Camp Moultrie, so long as they remain in the Territory of Florida, and to advance their proportional amount of the said annuity for the balance of the term stipulated for its payment in the treaty aforesaid; whenever they remove in compliance of the terms of this agreement.

In testimony wherefor, the Commissioner, James Gadsden, in behalf of the United States, and the undersigned Chiefs and Warriors have hereunto subscribed their names and affixed their seals.

Done at Tallahassee in the Territory of Florida, this eleventh day of October one thousand eight hundred and thirty-two, and of the Independence of the United States the fifty-seventh.

JAMES GADSDEN,
Commissioner, &c.

John Blunt,
O Saa-Hajo, or Davy,
Co-ha-thlock-co, or Cockrane.

WITNESSES—Wm. P. Duval, Supt. Stephen Richards, Interpreter, Robt. W. Williams. R. Lewis. Tho. Brown. James D. Westcott, Jr.

To the Indian names are subjoined marks.

REMOVAL OF SOUTHERN INDIANS TO INDIAN TERRITORY

Extract from Jackson's Seventh Annual Message to Congress December 7, 1835

(Richardson, ed. **Messages and Papers**, Vol. III, p 171ff)

Georgia's Indian policy, and the failure of Jackson to sustain the Supreme Court in its interpretation of the rights of the Indians, led to the plan removing the remaining Creeks, Cherokees, and other Indian tribes of the South to a reservation west of the Mississippi. This policy had been outlined by Jackson in his first message to Congress, and in 1830 Congress had appropriated half a million dollars for removal of the Indians to the west. In 1834 Congress created a special Indian Territory, and by a treaty of December 29, 1835, the Indians surrendered their lands east of the Mississippi in return for five million dollars, the expenses of removal, and land. See G. Foreman, Indian Removal; G. Foreman, Indians and Pioneers, ch. xxi; W. MacDonald, Jacksonian Democracy, ch. x.

Washington, December 7, 1835.

. . . The plan of removing the aboriginal people who yet remain within the settled portions of the United States to the country west of the Mississippi River approaches its consummation. It was adopted on the most mature consideration of the condition of this race, and ought to be persisted in till the object is accomplished, and prosecuted with as much vigor as a just regard to their circumstances will permit, and as fast as their consent can be obtained. All preceding experiments for the improvement of the Indians have failed. It seems now to be an established fact that they can not live in contact with a civilized community and prosper. Ages of fruitless endeavors have at length brought us to a knowledge of this principle of intercommunication with them. The past we can not recall, but the future we can provide for. Independently of the treaty stipulations into which we have entered with the various tribes for the usufructuary rights they have ceded to us, no one can doubt the moral duty of the Government of the United States to protect and if possible to preserve and perpetuate the scattered remnants of this race which are left within our borders. In the discharge of this duty an extensive region in the West has been assigned for their permanent residence. It has been divided into districts and allotted among them. Many have already removed and others are preparing to go, and with the exception of two small bands living in Ohio and Indiana, not exceeding 1,500 persons, and of the Cherokees, all the tribes on the east side of the Mississippi, and extending from Lake Michigan to Florida, have entered into engagements which will lead to their transplantation.

The plan for their removal and reestablishment is founded upon the knowledge we have gained of their character and habits, and has been dictated by a spirit of enlarged liberality. A territory exceeding in extent that relinquished has been granted to each tribe. Of its climate, fertility, and capacity to support an Indian population the representations are highly favorable. To these districts the Indians are removed at the expense of the United States, and with certain supplies of clothing, arms, ammunition and other indispensable articles; they are also furnished grautitously with provisions for the period of a year after their arrival at their new homes. In that time, from the nature of the country and of the products raised by them, they can subsist themselves by agricultural labor, if they choose to resort to that mode of life; if they do not they are upon the skirts of the great prairies, where countless herds of buffalo roam, and a short time suffices to adapt their own habits to the changes which a change of the animals destined for their food may require. Ample arrangements have also been made for the support of the schools; in some instances council houses and churches are to be erected, dwellings constructed for the chiefs, and mills for common use. Funds have been set apart for the maintenance of the poor; the most necessary mechanical arts have been introduced, and blacksmiths, gunsmiths, wheelwrights, millrights, etc., are supported among them. Steel and iron, and sometimes salt, are purchased for them, and plows and other farming utensils, domestic animals, looms, spinning wheels, cards, etc., are presented to them. And besides these beneficial arrangements, annuities are in all cases paid, amounting in some instances to more than $30 for each individual of the tribe, and in all cases sufficiently great, if justly divided and prudently expended, to enable them, in addition to their own exertions, to live comfortably. And as a stimulus for exertion, it is now provided by law that 'in all cases of the appointment of interpreters or other persons employed for the benefit of the Indians a preference shall be given to persons of Indian decent, if such can be found who are properly qualified for the discharge of the duties.'

Such are the arrangements for the physical comfort and for the moral improvement of the Indians. The necessary measures for their political advancement and for their separation from our citizens have not been neglected. The pledge of the United States has been given by Congress that the country destined for the residence of this people shall be forever 'secured and guaranteed to them.' A country west of Missouri and Arkansas has been assigned to them, into which the white settlements are not to be pushed. No political communities can be formed in that extensive region, except those which are established by the Indians themselves, or by the United States for them and with their concurrence. A barrier has thus been raised for their protection against the encroachment of our citizens, and guarding the Indians as far as possible from those evils which have brought them to their present condition. Summary authority has been given by laws to destroy all ardent spirits found in their country, without waiting the doubtful result and slow process of legal seizure. I consider the absolute and unconditional interdiction of this article among these people as the first and great step in their melioration. Halfway measures will answer no purpose. These can not successfully contend against the cupidity of the seller and the overpowering appetite of the buyer. And the destructive effects of the traffic are marked in every page of the history of our Indian intercourse . . .

RESOURCE SECTION

History and Government of Florida
Brevard, Caroline Mayr-dated 1904, 1919

The Militant South
Franklin, John Hope
Beacon Press, 1956

American: The People and Values
Wood, Leonard; Gabriel, Ralph;
Biller, Edward
Harcourt Brace Jovanovich, 1979, 2nd Ed.

Florida, The Long Frontier
Douglas, Marjory Stoneman
Harper & Row, 1967

La Florida
Copeland and Dovell
Steck-Vaughn Company, 1957

Confederate Military History
Volume I Secession and the Civil War
Volume XII Alabama and Mississippi
Confederate Publishing Company, 1866
Republished by The Blue & Grey Press

Journey into Wilderness
Motte, Jacob Rhett
University of Florida Press, 1963

The Unconquered Seminole Indian
Peithmann, Irvin M.
Outdoor Press, St. Petersburg, Fla., 1956

Notices of Florida and the Campaigns
Cohen, M.M.
Reprint University of Florida Press, 1964

The Florida Historical Quarterly: Volume 30 No. 1
The Florida Historical Society, July 1951

The War in Florida
Potter, Woodburne
Reprint Readex Microprint Corp., 1966

Observations Upon the Floridas
Vigmoles, Charles
Reprint the University of Florida Press 1977

The Battle of New Orleans
Chidsey, Donald Barr
Crown Publishers, Inc., New York, 1961

Documents of American History, 5th Edition
Commager, Henry Steel
Appleton-Century—Crofts, Inc. 1949

History of the United States
Ridpath, John Clark
Philips & Hunt, New York 1884

Our Republic
Forman, S.E.

The Century Company, New York, 1922

Salvery and Plantation Growth in Antebellum Florida
Smith, Julia Floyd
University of Florida Press, Gainesville, 1973

Time on the Cross
Fogel and Engerman
Little, Brown and Company, Boston, 1974

The Journal of Muscle Shoals History
Volume 3, 1975
Volume 4, 1976
Volume 6, 1978
Volume 7, 1979
University of North Alabama, Florence, Ala.

Fearless and Free
Walton, George
Bobbs-Merrill Company, Inc., 1977

Red Patriots
Coe, Charles K.
Reprint University of Florida, 1974

History of the Second Seminole War
Mahon, John K.
Univeristy of Florida Press, 1967

Florida Statutes Annotated—Vol. 24
The Harrison Company and West Publishing Co., 1944

Jefferson
Padover, Saul K.
Harcourt, Brace and Company, 1942

Hopes, Dreams and Promises
Schene, Michael G.
News Journal Corp, Daytona Beach, 1976

Florida, Pathways to Progress
Deans and Spears
The Graphic Language Corp, Tallahassee, Fl., 1979

Monographs from Historic Florida Militia School Kit

Population & Social Structure in Colonial St. Augustine

Daily Life in 18th Century St. Augustine

Craft Production in the Eighteen Century

Blacks in Colonial America, Joe Gray Taylor

Indentured Servants in America, Barbara Bigham

Outline for Gallegos House

Historical Report on the Pesode Burg—Pellicer Site, Overton G. Ganong